Understanding
the
Faith

from a Mennonite Perspective

A STUDY GUIDE

Helmut Harder

Published jointly by
CMBC Publications, Winnipeg, Manitoba
Faith & Life Press, Newton, Kansas
1997

CMBC Publications
600 Shaftesbury Blvd.
Winnipeg, Manitoba R3P 0M4

Faith & Life Press
718 Main Street
Newton, Kansas 67114

Cover: Gerald Loewen
adapted from a design by Gwen M. Stamm

Canadian Cataloguing in Publication Data

Harder, Helmut, 1934–

Understanding the faith from a Mennonite perspective

Study guide to accompany Confession of faith in a Mennonite perspective.

ISBN: 0-920718-57-4

1. Mennonites - Creeds. 2. General Conference Mennonite Church - Creeds. 3. Mennonite Church - Creeds. I. Title. II. Title: Confession of faith in a Mennonite perspective.

BX8124.H37 1997   238'.973   C97-920130-6

Copyright ©1997
Canadian Mennonite Bible College

Printed in Canada by
Friesens
Altona, Manitoba R0G 0B0

Contents

The *Confession of Faith in a Mennonite Perspective,* on which this study guide is based, was accepted by the General Conference Mennonite Church and the Mennonite Church in 1995 at their respective delegate meetings in Wichita Kansas.

Copies of the *Confession* can be purchased at Mennonite bookstores; or ordered from the publisher: Herald Press, 490 Dutton Drive, Waterloo, Ontario N2L 6H7; 616 Walnut Avenue, Scottdale, Pennsylvania 15683 (1-800-245-7894); or from Faith & Life Press, 600 Shaftesbury Blvd, Winnipeg, Manitoba R3P 0M4; 718 Main Street, Newton, Kansas 67114 (1-800-743-2484).

Preface

Confessions of faith are tightly worded statements of what the church believes. As such they should not be read quickly—each sentence invites deep reflection. As such they should be studied in company, in the church. Each statement of belief invites vigorous discussion and communal learning.

The *Confession of Faith in a Mennonite Perspective* is no exception. It too is a statement packed with scriptural truths and theological interpretation for our time. It too is written by and for the church.

Understanding the Faith is a study guide whose purpose is to help students of the Christian faith explore the contents of the *Confession of Faith in a Mennonite Perspective*. The twenty-four chapters of the study guide follow the twenty-four articles of the *Confession of Faith*. Each chapter contains key statements (in bold print) and Scripture references drawn from the articles of the *Confession. Understanding the Faith* should be used hand in hand with the *Confession of Faith,* and always within reach of the open Bible.

While this study guide is suitable for individual reading, it is written primarily for use in the church community. Christian faith and commitment find their true home in the company of committed believers. Here one's personal faith gains nurture and direction and one's desire for a life of peace and justice in the world find support. To this end may this book be helpful not only to those in the Mennonite church, but also those from other Christian traditions who wish to learn from the Mennonite way.

Helmut Harder
September 1997

*Faith is obedience to God and
the confidence in [God's] promise
through Jesus Christ.
Where this obedience is absent
there all confidence is false
and a deception.
This obedience must be genuine,
that is that heart, mouth and
deed coincide together.*

—Hans Denck

*Christ is truly a reconciliation
for the whole world;
neverthless, this does not benefit anyone,
except only those who recognize and
accept Him through faith. . . .
When one speaks of justification
through Christ,
one must also speak of that faith,
which cannot be without
works of repentance.*

—Michael Sattler

1
God

Is it possible for finite humans to understand an infinite Being who is shrouded in mystery? Can the creature comprehend the Creator? How can we know that God exists?

We believe that God exists and is pleased with all who draw near by faith. Our claim that God exists is made by faith. No one has ever seen God. Nor has anyone proved the existence of God for sure. We cannot get further in this life than to "believe that he exists" (Hebrews 11:6).

While no one has seen God, there are signs of God's reality all around. We marvel at God's "footprints" in the vast and magnificent universe. We are amazed at the intricate microcosmic detail of creation. We see the "image of God" reflected in humans (Genesis 1:27). We hear God's word proclaimed by preachers and taught by teachers.

Above all, we know God through Jesus Christ. Of him it was said: "No one has ever seen God. It is God the only Son, who is close to the Father's heart, who has made him known" (John 1:18). Jesus lived among humankind as the Son of God in human form. This revelation of God is recorded in the New Testament.

Amazingly, we have been given the capacity to draw near to God. We can think about God and speak to God in prayer. We can feel God's presence through intuition and in worship. People who were with Jesus of Nazareth when he walked upon the earth sensed that God had come near to them through this person. When we read what Jesus taught and did, and when we see and hear of persons in our day who reflect his life and teachings, we sense the nearness of God. In these ways we "draw near [to God] by faith" (Hebrews 11:6).

We worship the one holy and loving God who is Father, Son and Holy Spirit eternally. We approach God in an attitude of worship. This calls for submission and confession. We express submission by bowing our heads in humility or by extending our hands outward in the expectation that God's Holy Spirit will connect with us from beyond ourselves. We express confession by admitting we are sinners who need to be accepted by God just as we are. These expressions symbolize an attitude of heart and a commitment of the will.

In the centuries following New Testament times, the church developed the doctrine of the Trinity. In the New Testament there is reference to God as "Father, Son, and Holy Spirit." To early church leaders this three-fold concept provided the ingredients for a balanced view of God. The emphasis on "God the Father" pointed to a supreme authority. The attention to "God the Son" gave historical focus to God. The confession of "God the Holy Spirit" reminded Christians of the comforting nearness of God. But this does not mean there are three of them. God is one. The three "persons" represent the three ways God is known to us.

Beginning with Abraham and Sarah, God has called forth a people of faith. Community—people in relationship—is God's medium of revelation. God becomes known in and through community. We read in Genesis 12 how God called Abraham and Sarah to begin a new community of faith. Their trust in God influenced the relatives with whom they journeyed to the promised land of Canaan. Their faith also influenced their children and their children's children, from generation to generation. Evidently faith in God and knowledge of God are received and lived out in relationships with people of faith from one generation to another.

The community that was begun with Abraham and Sarah eventually, after many generations, became the community within which God's Son, Jesus of Nazareth, was born. But

Jesus did not limit himself to the Israelite community. His words and actions revealed that God wanted people of every nation to be included in the circle of God's people. This prepared the way for the church, a people from many nations. Now God had a new setting in which to become known.

We humbly acknowledge that God far surpasses human comprehension and understanding. As people of faith engage in the pilgrimage of life, not all mysteries about God are answered with clarity. Daily life brings many puzzling questions: If there is a God, why do bad things happen to good people? Will people ever learn to get along? Will there ever be enough to eat for all? Why is there so much pain in today's family? The questions keep coming.

Lest we become overwhelmed with unsolved questions about God and life, we should learn from the insights of Dietrich Bonhoeffer, the German theologian, whose life was ended in a Nazi prison camp. He reminds us in one of his letters from prison that God is there, not to rescue us from suffering and distress, but to accompany us in the midst of life's perplexities.

People sometimes say: "I can't believe in God! Look at all the suffering in the world!" Bonhoeffer points out that suffering does not disprove the existence of God. Rather, it emphasizes our need for God who desires to help us in the midst of suffering and to guide us through the valleys of life. God suffers with us.

God has spoken to humanity and related to us in many and various ways. The Bible addresses God with a rich variety of names and character references. The beginning of Psalm 91 provides a good example. God is named "the Most High," "the Almighty," "the Lord," "my fortress" and "my refuge" (91:1–2). Next God is compared to someone who warns us of a trap and delivers us from sickness (91:3). Then the Psalmist uses the example of an eagle and of soldier's armour to tell of

4 Understanding the Faith from a Mennonite Perspective

God's protective power (91:4). These are only a few of the countless names and descriptions for God in the Bible.

The gender of God is sometimes discussed and debated. Is God male? Female? Both? Neither? We begin by noting that while some names for God are gender-related (God as Father), many of the names for God and characteristics of God in the Bible are not concerned with gender. Names such as "the Most High" or "the God of peace" (Hebrews 13:20) or "I am" (Exodus 3:14) do not require us to think in terms of gender. Indeed, some depictions of God, such as Light (1 John 1:5) or Word (John 1:1), go beyond the idea of person. Yet these too belong to our knowledge of who God is.

Jesus addressed God as "Abba" (Father) and taught us to do the same (Matthew 6:9). "Abba" was a term of endearment in Jesus' day, something like "daddy." Jesus invites us to address God as "our Father in heaven." However, this usage does not determine the sexuality of God. Sexuality belongs to the created order, since we read that God created humans—both male and female—in the divine image (Genesis 1:27). While the father-image and many other this-worldly images are helpful for an understanding of God, it is Jesus Christ who best nurtures our understanding of God.

How fortunate that humans are endowed with tools of language and thought whereby to comprehend what is necessary for "a beginner's knowledge of God." Enough has been revealed to us about God that we can live by and act on. A hymn writer says: "We know enough, but not too much, to long for more."

God's awesome glory and enduring compassion are perfect in holy love. God is love. This is the most important statement we can make about God. Love is the operative word in our God-talk and our God-walk. This means we have our work cut out for us. How will people come to realize there is a God? John, the beloved disciple of Jesus wrote, "No one has ever seen God; if we love one another, God lives in us, and his love is perfected in us" (1 John 4:12). And again, "God is love, and those who abide in love abide in God, and God abides in them" (4:16b). We sing, "they'll know we are Christians by our love." Our love for one another provides a witness to the truth that God is love.

While the love of God is simple to express, it can sometimes be quite complex. On the one hand, God is awesome and powerful and eternal and infinite and judging and distant. On the other hand, God is compassionate and intimate and forgiving and patient and close to us. God is above the highest heavens; yet God dwells among us in Jesus Christ. So far away, and yet so near! To know the truth about God, we need to embrace both extremities, the distance of God and the nearness of God.

The love of God fits this expansive picture of God. On the one hand, God's inexhaustible and far-reaching love reaches around the entire universe. At the same time, God abides in love with each person in the midst of daily joys and sorrows. O the mystery of the love of God!

Questions for Discussion

1. Article 1 of the *Confession of Faith* identifies five central beliefs about God. Which of these are most important to you? Why?
2. The second sentence of Article 1 affirms our belief in the Trinity. How does the trinitarian confession about God keep us "on track" in our understanding of God?
3. What is your favourite "proof" for the existence of God?
4. How has the reality of God become evident in creation? In history? In the life of the church? In personal experience?
5. How does the emphasis on God as "Love" connect readily with a Mennonite understanding of faith and life?
6. Read up on biblical names for God using a concordance to the Bible, articles on this topic in Bible dictionaries and other resources. What do you learn from such a study?

Jesus Christ

What shall Christians confess about Jesus Christ? Was he divine? Was he human? Does the Old Testament speak of him? What is more important, his life or his death? Does Christ have a role in our future?

We believe in Jesus Christ, the Word of God become flesh. Turning from what we believe about God to what we believe about Jesus Christ, we move from mystery to revelation. Jesus Christ came to earth in human form to reveal God. "And the Word became flesh and lived among us, and we have seen his glory, the glory as of a father's only son, full of grace and truth" (John 1:14).

To regard Jesus as "the Word of God become flesh" requires a decision of faith. Many who saw and heard Jesus, accepted him as sent from God to fulfill the promise of a Saviour to the people of Israel. People crowded around him, and praised God for the divine power that flowed from his healing touch and the heavenly wisdom that he spoke. Disciples believed in him and sought to follow in his ways.

Some people misunderstood him completely. Leaders of religious insititutions thought he had come to upset their spiritual structures. Government officials regarded him as a threat to the stability of the country. While some confessed that his special powers were from God, others said he was driven by evil powers. These drastic misunderstandings contributed to his persecution and to a despicable death. "He came to what was his own, and his own people did not accept him" (John 1:11).

While some turned away from him because they could not believe he was from God, others turned away because they were not prepared for the kind of commitment for which he called. They were not ready to change their course of life in response to his invitation: "Take up your cross and follow me" (Matthew 16:24). Our believing comes to light in our commitment. Hans Denck, an early Anabaptist, said: "No one truly knows Christ except to follow him in life."

We confess Jesus as the Christ, the Messiah, through whom God has prepared the new covenant for all peoples. What's in a name? *Jesus* was the earthly name given him by his family. *Messiah* was a title some claimed for him, an Old Testament title for the religious and political leader of a people. Literally, it means "the anointed one," since the ceremony of installation included an anointing to indicate that the leader was chosen and blessed by God. The promise had been stated, especially through the prophets, that a Messiah would come who would, once and for all times, establish a permanent kingdom and rule the people with justice and peace. Matthew begins his account of the birth of Jesus with the words: "Now the birth of Jesus, the Messiah, took place in this way . . . ." (Matthew 1:18). The Greek translation of the title, Messiah, is *Christ*.

While Messiah is the most frequent title given Jesus, he received other names as well. All of them come from the Old Testament. The term *Son of God,* when applied to Christ, emphasized that he is an original Son of God, not an adopted Son. Those who follow Christ are in the "adopted" category (Romans 8:31). The term *Son of Man* connects Jesus with humanity and denotes him as the predestined representative of God's people. *Prince of Peace* and *Lion of Judah* were Old Testament names given him in recognition of his peaceful ways. He was called *Saviour* because he delivered us from sin and evil. The title *Lord* was added when he rose from the dead and ascended to heaven to reign with God. After his resurrection, it was a short step from his messiahship to the acclamation that Jesus is Lord. These names enrich our understanding of who he was, and is, and will be.

We accept Jesus Christ as the Saviour of the world. In the Old Testament, the term "salvation" or "to save" was used to describe experiences of rescue from deep trouble. The escape of the people of Israel from the pursuit of the Egyptians was called an experience of salvation. God was applauded as Saviour in that event. The people yearned for an earthly Saviour whom God would send to protect them from their enemies and save them from all ills.

Even before Jesus was born, his mother and his relatives hailed him as the coming *Saviour* of Israel and of all peoples. At his birth angels proclaimed the hope of "peace on earth" because of his arrival. John the Baptist introduced Jesus as "the Lamb of God who takes away the sin of the world" (John 1:29). Jesus himself spoke of his work as a worldwide mission to rescue the perishing: "For God so loved the world that he gave his only Son, so that everyone who believes in him may not perish but have eternal life" (John 3:16). Above all, his death on the cross and his resurrection from the dead established Jesus' saving power. John the disciple and apostle testified: "We have seen and do testify that the Father has sent his Son as the Saviour of the world" (1 John 4:14).

How does Jesus Christ become the Saviour *of the world*? He offers forgiveness of sins to all people regardless of a person's background, regardless of what they have or have not achieved, and regardless of how good or bad they have been. He makes no distinctions between people in terms of their race, their economic status, their physical condition or appearance, or any other factor. He is concerned with people's needs, whatever the need may be. His way of relating peacefully to people was inclusive and life-giving. He invites to a community which is open to all. His invitation is authentic and compelling because he lived what he preached.

Today, around the world, people proclaim Christ as the world's Saviour. We announce this truth not as an imposition or threat but as a loving invitation.

We acknowledge Jesus Christ as the only Son of God, the Word of God incarnate. The name, *Son of God,* is given to many persons in the Old Testament. It means, "belonging to God." In the New Testament, believers are named sons of God by adoption (Romans 8:31). The name is applied inclusively to both genders. Jesus Christ is singled out as the only original Son of God. Jesus has a foundational relationship with God. Our relationship derives from Jesus.

Jesus is the *Word of God* become flesh. In biblical thought, a word spoken or written is an integral part of the person who uttered the word. What you say is who you are. Words have the power to create new life beyond the person who speaks the words. Original words are originating words that bring forth new life. God uttered the creative word, and it became flesh in Jesus. In this sense, Jesus is the Word of God.

To be *incarnate* means to appear as an earthly human being. Early Christian doctrine referred to Jesus Christ as fully human and fully divine. Emphasis on the humanness of Jesus assures us that he identifies closely with the human condition, except that he was without sin. Emphasis on the divineness assures us that Jesus can be fully trusted as the Word of God incarnate. Theologians of the early church acknowledged that it is difficult to explain the full humanity and the full divinity of Jesus. The doctrine upholds the profound character of the person of Christ. It is important to know that this earthly person was, at the same time, the image of the invisible God.

We recognize Jesus Christ as the head of the church, his body. There are many dimensions to the person of Jesus Christ. Included in our understanding of Christ is his relationship to the church. The New Testament teaches that Jesus Christ is the *head of the church.* With Christ as the head, we understand the remaining members of the church to be on equal ground. "Speaking the truth in love, we must grow up in every way into him who is the head, into Christ" (Ephesians 4:15).

The church is *Christ's* body. "In him the whole structure is joined together and grows into a holy temple in the Lord" (2:21). This sounds somewhat idealistic. But it should be taken as an invitation to think deeply about the significance and the shape of the church as a community that holds great promise. What a privilege to take part in the ongoing formation of the extension of Christ's life on earth.

Persons who embrace the Christian faith are fortunate. They do not spend a lifetime floundering in a sea of opinions about the meaning of life. They do not experiment with all the choices of human behaviour offered in our day. Their self-understanding and their lifestyle are guided by the life and teachings of Jesus of Nazareth. They do not seek their saviours in political leaders or political parties, in sports heroes or rock stars, in quasi-religious leaders or philosophical gurus. In Jesus Christ, God disclosed the truth about existence and the way humans were meant to live. Jesus said: "I am the way, and the truth, and the life" (John 14:6). In the church they should find a caring community that keeps them centred in Jesus Christ. This community, when it is faithful, provides a model of Christ-likeness in and to the world.

We worship Jesus Christ as the one whom God has exalted and made Lord over all. When Jesus had completed his ministry on earth, which included his death and resurrection, he ascended into heaven. Now he has a special place at the right hand of God. As the *exalted Lord,* he is the guarantor of the promise of eternal life for all who are faithful to God. We believe in the coming again of Christ at the end of time, as he promised, and as indicated in the closing chapters of the last book of the Bible. While there is no guarantee that everyone will accept him, it will become evident to all people at the end of time that Jesus Christ is Saviour and Lord.

Questions for Discussion

1. Article 2 of the *Confession of Faith* identifies five central beliefs about Jesus Christ. Find Scripture passages which support each of these beliefs.
2. Which of these beliefs do you find easiest to understand? Which ones call for further study and discussion?
3. Explain in your own words what it means that Jesus Christ is the Word of God incarnate.
4. Find biblical texts which support the emphasis on Jesus Christ as the head and cornerstone of the church. What difference does this emphasis make for the worship and work of the church community?
5. How would you explain the reality of Jesus Christ to a person who has not heard of him or who does not believe that Jesus is central to an understanding of God?

3

Holy Spirit

Christians confess the Holy Spirit as the third person of the Trinity. Why is it important to believe in the Holy Spirit? How can we know the Spirit? How can we tell the difference between the true Holy Spirit and false spirits of our age? What do we believe about the Holy Spirit?

We believe in the Holy Spirit, the eternal Spirit of God, who dwelled in Jesus Christ. To confess that we believe in the Holy Spirit is to claim that God is active in the life-process. Spirit-language and Spirit-awareness provide a bridge between God's action and human acts of life in faith.

Thankfully, we know about the Holy Spirit, the third person of the Trinity. If we knew only of God, the Almighty One or the Father, we might think of God only as a distant divine authoritative being who sits high above the universe. If we knew only God as the Son, we might think of God only as a historical figure who was among us for a brief thirty years some 2,000 years ago. Knowing God as Holy Spirit, we are assured that God is near to us in a continuing way day by day. The Holy Spirit as the eternal Spirit of God is always with us.

In early Christian theology there was debate about how the Holy Spirit fits into the divine scheme of things. The point of the argument is worth mentioning. The hard question was this: Does the Holy Spirit depend only on God the Father, the first person of the Trinity, for its origin and activity? Or does the Holy Spirit also depend on the second person, the Son? What does it mean that the Holy Spirit dwelled in Jesus Christ?

Suppose a person who claimed to be possessed by the Holy Spirit blew up a planeload of military personnel associated with the enemies of his country. Why did he do it? Perhaps by some stretch of the imagination he insisted that God told him to; or he used an Old Testament story to justify the act, thereby claiming to be in line with the Spirit of God. However, the act would be contrary to the Spirit of Jesus. Jesus spoke against retaliation toward enemies. The person could not claim to be inspired by the Holy Spirit since the Holy Spirit is the Spirit of Jesus.

We believe that "the work of the Holy Spirit since Christ's exaltation always conforms to Jesus Christ" (*Confession of Faith in a Mennonite Perspective,* 19). Jesus said of the Spirit: "All that the Father has is mine. For this reason I say that he [the Spirit] will take what is mine and declare it to you" (John 16:15).

Through the Spirit of God, the world was created; prophets and writers of Scripture were inspired. The dynamics of life pervade the entire universe. Balmy breezes and strong winds blow persistently upon the face of the vast earth. A sea of humanity endures as thousands of people are born and thousands die every minute. Countless stars scattered over incomprehensible space and time are enlivened and lighted by a relentless flow of energy. Is all this life driven by wild surging power? By a natural inbuilt and predictable evolution of things? The Bible claims that life originates and is sustained by the Spirit of God.

"Spirit" is the English translation of the Hebrew word, *ruach,* which also means "wind" and "breath." Wind has a wide range of functions. For example, it parches the land, and it brings refreshing rain. It works destruction but also restoration. A strong wind is a sign of power, at times a sign of confusion.

The spirit of God came as wind (Genesis 1:2) and breath/speech (1:3); and the world was created. Breath is the carrier of words that emanate from the mouth of a person. Breath is the sign of life. Death is synonymous with the cessation of breathing as the spirit departs from a person. "Spirit" is also used to speak of a person filled with godly character, as when a leader is endowed with the spirit of wisdom (Deuteronomy 34:9).

The imagery of the Spirit of God pervades the biblical story. The world is created by the wind/spirit of God and by God's speech/breath (Genesis 1:1–3). Prophets spoke powerful words of God which created historical events. Scriptures were written as though God-breathed, and then miraculously preserved. Jesus was conceived, baptized, tempted, and sustained in life and death by the power of the Holy Spirit.

At Pentecost, God began to pour out the Spirit on all flesh and to gather the church from among many nations. After Jesus' ascension the disciples and others were gathered in Jerusalem for the Pentecost festival. There the Holy Spirit came upon them, accompanied by "a sound like the mighty rush of a violent wind, and . . . divided tongues, as of fire" (Acts 2:2–3). Then a miracle: people spoke in languages other than their own and heard of God's mighty deeds in their own native tongue.

The meaning of this sign was clear. God's Spirit is poured out on all flesh. The Gospel of Christ is for all nations and includes all genders and all classes of people (Acts 2:8–11, 17–21). "There is no longer Jew or Greek, there is no longer slave or free, there is no longer male or female; for all of you are one in Christ Jesus" (Galatians 3:28). The Old Testament focus on the choice of one nation to prepare the way for the Messiah had a purpose but the age of the Spirit is now upon us.

The Pentecost miracle paves the way for the Christian church throughout all ages. The Pentecost church is a public church, open to all people from many nations and from all sectors of life. Everyone is welcome to hear the Christian message and to join in Christian community. The gifts of the Spirit are available to all. The fruits of the Spirit are in evidence among all. It sometimes appears that only a miracle could move the church from disarray to unity. The Spirit has effected the miracle of unity and peace in the past, and can do so again.

The Holy Spirit calls people to repentance, convicts them of sin, and leads into the way of righteousness. We have a tendency to become set in our ways. We develop habits and we become firm about our opinions. At worst we completely close ourselves off to the advice of others and harden our hearts. This mindset spells trouble if the direction chosen or the opinion held is destructive of the good purposes of life and contrary to the will of God. Then the only solution is to admit our wrong-headedness and begin anew.

When people take a critical look at wrong attitudes and actions and become convinced of their sin, the Holy Spirit is calling them to repentance. To repent and invite God's spirit into our lives, we need to become "poor in spirit" (Matthew 5:3). This is only the beginning of the work of the Spirit. If the person makes the full turn-around and wills to do what is right, the Holy Spirit opens the way of righteousness. The Holy Spirit works in and through us if and when we open ourselves to the working of the Spirit in the ongoing course of life.

The Holy Spirit enables our life in Christian community. It is of great importance that we respect the Holy Spirit in our life together in the church. We come into Christian community with a human spirit. That is good and welcome. Each of us makes a vital personal and unique contribution to the complex dynamic of the congregation. But even in the best of situations the human spirit is fraught with temptations to self-centredness, materialism, irresponsibility, and the like. When we allow the human spirit to bask in God's Holy Spirit, we become pliable and teachable and open to spiritual formation. The apostle Paul challenges the church to aspire to "the unity of the Spirit in the bond of peace" (Ephesians 4:3).

When Jesus took leave of his disciples before making his way to the cross, he promised to send the Holy Spirit as an abiding presence in his place. The Spirit would remind the disciples of his teachings, comfort them in times of suffering,

*Just as the breath determines the word
   and gives it shape and sound,
so the breath, wind and spirit of God
   makes the word living and
   active within us and
   leads us into all truth.
We believe that the Holy Spirit . . .
   teaches, directs and instructs us,
   assures us that we are children of God,
   and makes us one with God.*
                              —Peter Riedeman

and give assurance of an eternal future with God. Christians today are connected to Jesus Christ through the Holy Spirit. To know the Spirit in this way requires a deep and continuing relationship with God.

Sometimes Christians try to restrict the work of the Spirit to one kind of human activity. Some think that the Spirit resides only in the leadership of the church. Some think that only persons who have had a one-time born-again experience have the Spirit. Others think that you have the Holy Spirit only if you are baptized in a specific way.

In the Corinthian church there were some who thought speaking in tongues is the evidence that a person has the Spirit. The apostle Paul corrected this impression by making two points. First, the Spirit is expressed in a great variety of gifts and activities (1 Corinthians 12:4–11). Second, the most important activity of the Spirit is love (1 Corinthians 13).

The spirit of love in Christian community originates in the Spirit of God and is driven by the ever-renewing Holy Spirit. "God's love has been poured into our hearts through the Holy Spirit that has been given to us" (Romans 5:5). Spirit-given love is radical in its expression because it loves in the spirit of Jesus. The story of the Good Samaritan illustrates the point (Luke 10:25–37). Incarnate love goes out of its way to become a neighbour to the one in need. To love is to act in the spirit of the Good Samaritan and in the spirit of Jesus' advice in the Sermon on the Mount: "Give to everyone who begs from you, and do not refuse anyone who wants to borrow from you" (Matthew 5:42). The spirit of love also revises the worldly understanding of justice. In accordance with the Spirit of God, justice is applied in protecting the helpless and showing mercy to those in trouble.

Questions for Discussion

1. Identify five aspects of belief in the Holy Spirit that come to light in Article 3 of the *Confession of Faith*. What happens if you leave

out one or another of these aspects?

2. Why is it important to focus our understanding of the work of the Holy Spirit on the Spirit's presence in Jesus?

3. What did the experience at Pentecost (Acts 1–2) teach believers about the work of the Holy Spirit?

4. Read 1 Corinthians 12, 13 and 14 to discover New Testament learnings about the work of the Holy Spirit.

5. The church desires and aspires to "the unity of the Spirit in the bond of peace" (Ephesians 4:3). What practical attitudes do Christians in the church need to "put on" to achieve the goal of unity and peace?

6. Explore the work of the Holy Spirit as it motivates the Christian call to act in a spirit of love and of justice.

4

Scripture

The Bible is in a class by itself. It is the most translated book of all times. Thousands of new books are published in the world each year. But the Bible outlasts and outsells them all. What is the role of the Bible for Christian faith and for the church?

We believe that all Scripture is inspired by God through the Holy Spirit for instruction in salvation and training in righteousness. Our denominational ancestors, the Anabaptists of the sixteenth century, took the Bible very seriously. They based their lives on what they found there. While many church leaders of their day appealed to church traditions and political structures, the Anabaptists appealed to Scripture.

In the 1520s in the city of Zurich a group of young adults came to new understandings of biblical truths. They concluded from their studies of Scripture that baptism is for believers, not for infants, and that the Lord's Supper is a fellowship meal, not a miracle in which bread and wine are changed to the flesh and blood of Christ. They understood that when there is a difference between what the rulers of the country require and what the Lord requires, they must obey the Lord. They were willing to suffer and die for the truth they discovered in the Bible.

Since traditional church leaders and political authorities had condemned anabaptist views, they could not rely on the usual persons in authority—bishops and kings—to assure them they were doing what was right. So they turned to the Scriptures. Here they found the much-needed assurance that they were included in God's circle of grace as revealed in Jesus Christ.

The Anabaptists had a high regard for the Bible. But they did not worship or make an idol of it. God was their authority. The Holy Spirit was their inspiration. The Scriptures provide a medium through which God prepares our hearts for faith and clears our heads to obey the will of God.

While the Bible contains many details, it answers the two most basic questions of life: What shall we believe? and, How shall we live? God's plan of salvation in Jesus Christ is the biblical answer to the first question. The biblical way of living righteously among all people is God's answer to the second question. To find these answers in the Bible requires diligent instruction and training.

We believe that God was at work through the centuries in the process by which the books of the Old and New Testament were inspired and written. My childhood introduction to the scope of the Bible came with the Sunday school assignment to learn and recite aloud the names of the 39 books of the Old Testament and the 27 books of the New Testament. It gave me satisfaction to memorize the entire sequence. It also gave me a sense of the magnitude and breadth of the Bible. I learned to appreciate the Bible as a volume of books, with different writers and various kinds of literature. I was impressed.

It is no small miracle that the Bible was brought together in one volume and that it has been preserved throughout the centuries to the present day. God must have watched over the process! The Old Testament involved numerous writers and communities of writers. At least ten writers were involved in formulating the New Testament into words. Besides these original writers, communities of writers copied and recopied the manuscripts, and archivists zealously preserved and guarded the manuscripts, sometimes hiding them from those who would destroy them. In many ways God prepared and preserved the Word. The greatest miracle is the story itself, recorded in the Bible. God works in creation and through individuals and communities to carry out God's purposes.

We accept the Bible as the Word of God written. Sometimes we call the Bible the "Word of God," as though regarding the paper and the ink of the Bible as somehow divine. It is not wrong to refer to the Bible as the Word of God. But in doing so we must be careful not to lose sight of the *living* Word of God pointed to by the written and printed words.

Prior to the written record, God spoke to and through people. The Word of the Lord was given through Moses, through kings and prophets, and through the apostles. God spoke through the mouth of his Son, Jesus, as he taught and preached (Hebrews 1:1–3). God's Word came through countless events, such as the act of creation and the baptism of Jesus.

Supremely, God spoke through a person, Jesus Christ, who was called "the Word" (John 1:1,14). These various forms of the living Word of God form the background for the Bible, the Word of God written. The key which unlocks the mysteries of the written word is Jesus Christ. All Scripture, both the Old and New Testaments, need to be interpreted in harmony with the revelation of God in Christ.

The purpose of the Bible is to lead people to encounter the living Word. That is why Jesus warned his hearers: "You search the scriptures, because you think that in them you have eternal life, and it is they that bear witness to me; yet you refuse to come to me that you may have life" (John 5:39–40). In themselves, the Scriptures are a testimony about God and about humanity's relationship to God. Their purpose is to invite us to a personal encounter with Christ.

We acknowledge the Scriptures as the authoritative source and standard for preaching and teaching about faith and life. Among the earliest martyrs in Anabaptist history was a former priest, Michael Sattler. He was a leader in writing the earliest known Anabaptist Confession of Faith, the Schleitheim Confession (1927). Sattler was placed on trial for his faith. The testimony at his trial bears witness to his undaunting devotion to the Scriptures.

The *Martyrs Mirror* records nine charges against Sattler. The first accusation was that Sattler and his followers were not obedient to the Emperor. The ninth accusation was that Sattler had said that "if the Turks should invade the country, no resistance should be offered them" (Thieleman J. van Braght, *Martyrs Mirror,* 416). That is, he held to the biblical teaching that you should love your enemies.

In his defence, Sattler said, simply: "I am not aware that we have acted contrary to the Gospel and the Word of God; I appeal to the words of Christ" (*Martyrs Mirror,* 417). In response to one of the many verbal attacks against him during the court session, Sattler replied: "I am not sent to judge the Word of God; we are sent to bear witness to it . . . (and) we are ready to suffer for the Word of God . . . unless we be dissuaded from it by the Scriptures." When the judge said: "The hangman will convince you," Sattler answered: "I appeal to the Scriptures" (418). Thereupon Michael Sattler was delivered to the executioner, under whose supervision he was tortured and burned to ashes.

The Mennonite church's zeal for the authority of Scripture was forged by events such as this. Not only men, but also women, gave their lives for the claim that the Scriptures are the fully reliable and trustworthy standard for Christian faith and life. Sattler's wife and other believers, both women and men, were also subjected to threats by the authorities and eventually drowned or killed in other ways.

The Bible is the essential book of the church. The church is the guardian of the Bible. The church is entrusted with its faithful translation and its preservation. The church also sees to it that the Bible is interpreted correctly. The church is responsible for sharing the Bible with those who have not heard or read it. The church is "the keeper of the Book."

At the same time, the Bible is the guardian of the church. The Bible takes care of the church. The Bible nurtures the life and faith of the church. It is the church's food. It is also the essential spiritual food of the individual believer and of the

Christian family. The ways and words of God, which are recorded in the Bible, provide "a lamp to my feet and a light to my path" (Psalm 119:105).

For this to happen, the Bible needs to occupy a prominent place in the faith community. A significant number in the congregation should have a breadth of knowledge and depth of understanding of the Scriptures. The Bible is an authoritative reference book for preaching and teaching, for worship and witness. In spirit and in practice, the church defines itself as a people gathered around the Bible. In this setting, the Bible is not an end in itself but an instrument that points to the living God and provides entrance for the Holy Spirit into the church.

While there is a place for persons simply to share unprepared opinions about "what this verse means to me," Bible study needs to go deeper. A patient study of Scripture passages in their original context yields reliable nourishment for life and faith. A comparison of Scripture texts with related texts often clarifies the meaning. The church setting—which includes the congregation, Bible study groups, seminars, Bible colleges, seminaries, conference gatherings—is the place where individual understandings and interpretation of Scripture are tested.

Questions for Discussion

1. What are some characteristics of the Anabaptist-Mennonite attitude to the Bible? What led to this perspective?
2. The Bible is often referred to as the "Word of God." How do you look at the Bible? In what other ways does the Bible itself apply the term, "Word of God?"
3. Can anyone interpret the Bible as they wish? Or are there limits to how the Bible gets interpreted? By whom are they established? What are the standards?
4. Which of the Scripture texts listed on page 22 of the *Confession of Faith* appeal most to you? Why?
5. Sometimes the Bible is referred to as a mirror. Is this a good metaphor for you? For your congregation? How does the Bible apply to you in your everyday life?

Creation and Divine Providence

We believe, on the basis of biblical revelation, that the universe was brought into being by God. The Bible begins this way: "In the beginning God created . . . ." (Genesis 1:1). This is a bold claim about how the world came to be. What is the consequence of believing that God is the originator of the universe and all that is in it?

We believe that God created the heavens and the earth and all that is in them. First, to believe in God the Creator means that the universe belongs to the Lord, not to us. Psalm 24:1 says: "The earth is the Lord's and all that is in it, the world and those who live in it." The created world is not ours to own and to do with as we please. Everything we are and see and touch belongs to God.

Second, to believe in God the Creator calls us to receive life and its environment with thanksgiving and respect. It is a privilege and a responsibility to live and learn, to work and play, in the midst of the created order.

Third, to believe in God as Creator implies that we will work as stewards of what has been entrusted to us for a time. We are caretakers of God's universe. Created materials have been given into our hands for the purpose of sharing so as to enhance our life and the life of others.

Fourth, to recognize God as Creator means we will distinguish between the Maker and what is made. We worship the Creator; we do not worship objects in nature or things manufactured by people. The temptation to equate things with God borders on idolatry. Humans are created in God's image; that is, they reflect God. Humans are not God. We will not regard as divine anything that God created or that humans make.

Fifth, to believe God created the universe is to view the created order as having the potential for good. A little boy said: "God didn't make no junk!" Obviously not everything that happens in and to the environment is good. We live in a world where there is brokenness and sin. But we know God made creation for good and wishes good to come of it. That's a challenge to us.

We believe that God preserves and renews what has been made. The creation account in Genesis 1 sounds a positive note, moving from a sequence of five daily affirmations that creation is "good" to a sixth climactic announcement that creation is "very good." The sixth pronouncement follows the creation of humans. While bad things happen to people on this earth and while evil persists in many places, the created world is not bad or evil by definition. God, who is good, creates people for good.

Nor does the theme of the goodness of creation die in Genesis 3. In Psalm 104 we read: "O Lord, my God, you are very great. You are clothed with honor and majesty. You set the earth on its foundations, so that it shall never be shaken. O Lord, how manifold are your works! In wisdom you make them all; the earth is full of your creatures" (vv.1,5,24). Matthew 6:28 records Jesus' words: "Consider the lilies of the field, how they grow; they neither toil nor spin, yet I tell you, even Solomon in all his glory was not clothed like one of these."

We believe that the universe has been called into being as an expression of God's love and sovereign freedom alone. Whether on purpose or by default, most people come to terms in one way or another with the created universe that surrounds them. Some search horoscopes and the stars for security and for predictable life patterns. Some allow themselves to be swayed back and forth between the unpredictable forces of good and evil, revelling in the mystery of their eventual fate. Some people put their trust in science, hoping to conquer the uncertainties of life through the advancements of technology, even in their lifetime. Some amass fortunes (or dream of doing so) in the hope of buying ultimate solutions to whatever would threaten them in life. Some simply give in to an irresponsible attitude: "Eat, drink, and be merry, for tomorrow we shall die!"

Christians position themselves differently in the created universe than any of the above. We believe that God intended the universe to provide a positive environment for life. God has a purpose for creation. The world was created by God in wisdom and in love. This is shown in the way the created world makes sufficient provision for daily needs. It is of great comfort in troubling times to know that our life and our world were created as an expression of God's love.

It should be obvious that we did not invent ourselves or bring the world into being. Nor are we the key players in sustaining the universe. We are capable of influencing directions of nature somewhat in positive or destructive directions. We are able to influence our own personal lives in healthy or unhealthy directions. But these are only micro-adjustments within a macrocosm. God is sovereign ruler of the universe.

Happily, we can affirm a Creator who wishes the singular good of creation. We do not perceive God to be at war with forces of evil in a battle whose end is not yet determined. The universe was not created as an arena where humans should skirmish to see who relishes victory and who suffers loss, but as a place where all can enjoy expressions of God's love. While there are evil forces in the world, God is the victor.

Our life is in God's hands. This means God is free to give life and to take life. God is the Alpha and the Omega, the beginning and the end. Believing this, we entrust our lives to a faithful Creator.

We acknowledge that God sustains creation in both continuity and change. The Creator's hand is evident in the continuities of life. We readily thank God for the predictable seasons that unfold in the course of the year, bringing seedtime and harvest. We acknowledge God's blessing in and through the regularity of worship Sunday after Sunday. We depend on God to continue patterns of growth and development in the future as we have enjoyed them in the past.

It is more difficult to recognize God's nearness in the discontinuities of life. Where is God when violence breaks out in an African nation, destroying thousands of innocent lives? Where is God when wind and hail destroy the crops in our community? Can we still claim that God sustains creation when catastrophes come upon us? We believe that God will not allow the created order to collapse. While the forces of sin and evil continue all around us, the forces of preservation and renewal are stronger. In Romans 1:20 we read: "Ever since the creation of the world his eternal power and divine nature, invisible though they are, have been understood and seen through the things he has made."

It is quite remarkable that the human race has not self-destructed. Genesis records several occasions when humans were on the verge of collapse. Adam and Eve make a near-disastrous attempt to live without reference to God (Genesis 2–3). They realize their vulnerability ("nakedness") and accept God's discipline. The Lord God sends them from the place where they had courted destruction with a gesture of grace that protected them from their self-styled designs. They were denied access to the temptation (the tree of the knowledge of good and evil) that had led them to presume they could disassociate themselves from their Creator and Sustainer.

God responded in a similar way when Cain murdered his brother Abel (Genesis 4), when people in Noah's time spurned God's plan for morality (Genesis 6–9), and when misguided construction workers attempted to build a tower from which to rule the world in God's place (Genesis 11). In the aftermath of these human temptations, again and again, God's creative purposes and promises were upheld. The ultimate event of this occurred when the attempt of persons to get rid of Jesus was thwarted by his glorious resurrection from death.

We are called to respect the natural order of creation and to entrust ourselves to God's care and keeping, whether in adversity or plenty. We approach the natural order with respect. The world of nature hangs on a thin thread. Think of the fragility of the insect world. Consider the absolute dependence of an infant child. Be reminded of the crucial role the vulnerable ozone layer contributes to our well-being. We need to tread carefully on the face of the earth lest we trample down and snuff out the very things that are meant to sustain us. Our call is for humility toward God and responsibility for the earth.

The rule of thumb is: If you take care of the earth, it will care for you. God has created a world of plenty with enough shelter and food for each and for all. But we must treat what has been given into our hands with stewardly care. Most often it is a question of equitable sharing and just distribution. People with plenty need to share with people in adversity. The apostle Paul encouraged the Corinthians to share with one another, so that "the one who had much did not have too much, and the one who had little, did not have too little" (2 Corinthians 8:15).

We need to be reminded daily that God sustains life. The Creator did not abandon the world once it was brought into being. Even though sin and evil damaged the original creation, God is still "working salvation in the earth" (Psalm 74:12).

The lesson to learn from this is that God cares for us. We need not resort to quick-handed and impatient solutions when adversity comes our way. We do not find our ultimate security in technology or in military protection. We trust God's providential care which requires that we take a long-range view that includes life beyond death.

Questions for Discussion

1. Which of the five implications of belief in God as creator, discussed on pages 24 and 25, need to be emphasized in our day?
2. Do you think there is a limit to God's commitment to preserve and renew creation? Are humans capable of partially or fully destroying what has been created?
3. What are the implications of the biblical teaching that the universe is created as an expression of God's love and sovereignty?
4. What did Jesus teach about creation and divine providence?
5. "If you take care of the earth, it will take care of you." How have you experienced this?

The Creation and Calling of Human Beings

The Bible says that people were created by God: "So God created humankind" (Genesis 1:27). The Creator "formed man from the dust of the ground, and breathed into his nostrils the breath of life; and man became a living being" (2:7). What a grand and glorious heritage for the human race and for each of us individually. Our factory trademark reads: "Made by God." What does it mean to confess that we are God's creation?

We believe that human beings were created good, in the image of God. In Genesis 1 we read that humans were created good. To be called "good" means to be blessed with the ability to do good. A good person is one who can make a wise choice in an ethical situation. A good person is one who is capable of relating to God and following in God's ways. To be called good is a statement about the human potential when properly directed. Human beings were not made to be bad, but to be good.

What does it mean to be created in the image of God? Students of the Bible are not certain what all is meant by the "image of God." It certainly includes the ability to commune with God and with others, and to bear God-given responsibilities in the created order. According to Genesis 1, God assigns the care of the earth to humankind. This implies that men and women are capable of conversing with God about human responsibility. This is the image of God at work within us.

Both male and female are created in the image of God. We read: "So God created humankind in his image, in the image of God he created them, male and female he created them"

(Genesis 1:27). This speaks of equal status before God and mutual blessing for male and female.

Biblical interpreters have also taken this to mean that femaleness and maleness are distinctions that apply on the human level but not within the divine Being. God is able to be reflected in both genders. Yet God is more than either male or female. God is Spirit. God is Love. God is transcendent Being.

We have been made stewards to subdue and care for creation. Man and woman are given an enormous and awesome assignment: "Be fruitful and multiply, and fill the earth and subdue it; and have dominion over . . . the fish . . . the birds . . . and over every living thing that moves upon the earth" (Genesis 1:28); "And the Lord God took the man and put him in the garden of Eden to till it and keep it" (2:15). Psalm 8:6 says: "You have given them dominion over the works of your hands; you have put all things under their feet."

Having created humans with response-ability, the Lord God proceeds to assign tasks. The assignment to "subdue" creation and have "dominion" over it is not a blank cheque. We may not do whatever we wish to the sea, the sky and the earth. The biblical emphasis is on caring for the created world. God gave permission to make use of creation for daily needs and to enjoy its beauty and fruitfulness.

We care for the earth on God's behalf. We are the stewards (householders, caretakers); God is the owner. It is a glorious privilege to be entrusted with God's creation: "What are human beings that you are mindful of them . . . ? You have made them a little lower than God, and have crowned them with glory and honor. You have given them dominion over the works of your hands; and put all things under their feet" (Psalm 8:5–6).

The second chapter of Genesis (Genesis 2:4b–25) sheds further light on our stewardship (see especially (2:8–9,15). The Lord God creates humans and places them in the midst of a garden of trees. There is an abundance of two kinds of trees: "trees that are pleasant to the sight and good for food" (v.9).

The garden supplies all that is necessary for life: beauty and sustenance.

But the wisdom to live in the midst of creation in a God-pleasing way does not come automatically. To guide and remind them of the principle that should shape the course of life, the Lord God plants two trees in the midst of the garden: the tree of life and the tree of the knowledge of good and evil (Genesis 2:9). The first of these two trees, the tree of life, is a reminder that life has its source in God alone. The second, the tree of the knowledge of good and evil, is a symbol that God alone is the source of wisdom. Wisdom is to know what is good (right) and what is evil (wrong). Stewardship of the earth can be carried out responsibly for God if and when God is recognized as the source of life and wisdom.

When we begin to take life into our own hands, doing as we please with it, we are heading down the wrong pathway. When we position ourselves as the source and centre of wisdom, we are headed for trouble. We cannot function responsibly on God's behalf if we operate in a self-centred way.

This wrong direction is indicated in Romans 1:21–23: "For though they knew God, they did not honor him as God or give thanks to him, but they became futile in their thinking, and their senseless minds were darkened. Claiming to be wise, they became fools, and they exchanged the glory of the immortal God for images resembling a mortal human being or birds or four-footed animals or reptiles."

God's will from the beginning has been for women and men to live in mutually helpful relationships with each other. The Bible directs us to the high ideal of living in mutually helpful relationships with each other. The basis for serving one another is laid when humans are created as equals under one Lord who alone is worthy of honour and authority. For the rest, humans are placed in mutual (even) relationship with one other.

The first and most important biblical sample of human community is the relationship of male and female. According to Genesis 1:27, God created both male and female in the divine image, not male only or female only. Both genders have mutual status before God and stand on common ground with one another. In Genesis 2 we read that the woman was created from the rib of the man, and that the woman was "a helper as his partner" (2:20). Nothing in this story means that the woman was of lesser status or worth. They are partners.

A mutual rather than dominant relationship between male and female is supported in the New Testament. In Ephesians 5:21 we read: "Be subject to one another out of reverence for Christ." In the Letter to the Galatians the apostle Paul says, on the basis of the practice of baptism (Galatians 3:27) that "there is no longer male and female; for all of you are one in Christ Jesus" (3:28).

Some Christians are confused by Genesis 3:16 where the Lord God says to the woman that "he [the husband] shall rule over you." But this describes a situation of sin and punishment, not of redemption. Persons redeemed in Christ are called to uphold the order of redemption, not of brokenness.

We are grateful that God patiently preserves humanity and faithfully remains with us even through death. We believe that God sustains humanity, even in and through death. God's preserving care for humanity is evidenced in the continuous succession of the generations of humankind through many centuries. God's care is shown and established in the promise of life after death, based on the resurrection of Jesus Christ. The apostle Paul offers an enthusiastic affirmation of God's sustaining love: "For I am convinced that neither death, nor life, nor angels, nor rulers, nor things present, nor things to come, nor powers, nor height, nor depth, nor anything else in all creation, will be able to separate us from the love of God in Christ Jesus our Lord" (Romans 8:38).

Death is a fact of life. It comes in many forms. There is progressive death in the sense that all of us experience gradual death every day as we advance in years from infancy on. There is instant death, which occurs all too frequently in our violent world. We can also distinguish between physical death and the death of a broken relationship. Broken relationships can occur on the human level between friends. They can also occur on the spiritual level in a relationship with God.

In the second creation account there is a reference to death. Here death refers to the potential death (breakdown) of Adam's relationship with God: "And the Lord God commanded the man: 'You may freely eat of every tree of the garden; but of the tree of the knowledge of good and evil you shall not eat, for in the day that you eat of it you shall die'" (Genesis 2:16–17).

The death of the relationship between God and humans hinges on the tree of the knowledge of good and evil. This tree, placed in the midst of the garden of Eden, stood as a reminder that the Creator intended humankind to look to the Lord God for wisdom. God would reveal to humans what was good and what was evil, and would give strength and grace to make right choices based on divine wisdom.

But first man and woman ate of the tree of the knowledge of good and evil. That is, they decided to take the situation into their own hands. They presumed to be able to make wise choices based on their own human perspective and serving their own self-interest. They left God out of the picture entirely. In this way they became gods unto themselves.

This move spells disaster. We don't realize our God-given potential and goals in life if we rely primarily on ourselves. Selfishness and pride take over eventually if not immediately. The Lord God expressed disappointment that Adam and Eve fell into the trap of relying on their own wisdom, thus breaking their lifeline with God. Yet God gave humankind another chance.

We believe that the image of God in all its fullness has been revealed and restored in Jesus Christ. With the entrance of sin into the world, the image of God was tarnished although not lost. We believe that Jesus Christ came to earth to restore the image of God among us. Adam and Eve, as the original bearers of the image of God, lost the privilege of bearing the fullness of the image. Jesus reinstated the image of God among humankind. "He is the image of the invisible God, the firstborn of all creation; for in him all things in heaven and on earth were created" (Colossians 1:15).

We find our true humanity once again in Christ. The New Testament speaks of a new creation: "So if anyone is in Christ, there is a new creation; everything old has passed away; see, everything has become new" (2 Corinthians 5:17). In Christ the image of God is restored in us.

Questions for Discussion

1. What is meant when we read in Genesis 1 that the creation of all things, including humans, was "good?"
2. What are the implications of the biblical teaching that both men and women were created in the image of God? (Genesis 1:27)
3. Explore the meaning of the trees in Genesis 2:4–25. What instruction do they offer concerning our relationship to God and to the environment?
4. Discuss the responsibility of Christians in the light of the biblical emphasis on relationships and community as it comes to light in the opening chapters of the Bible.
5. Reflect on the meaning of 2 Corinthians 5:17. What does it mean that in Christ we are a new creation?

Sin

Sin is not a popular subject for us moderns. It gets us quickly into judgmental and negative talk. We would rather concentrate on the good things that are happening. So when people make mistakes, and need to find ultimate reasons for failure, they tend to say: "The devil made me do it!" or "It was fate!" or "I was born bad!" or "Just a little slip." But that's not good enough. We need to come to grips with the reality of sin. Where should we begin?

We confess that, beginning with Adam and Eve, humanity has disobeyed God, given way to the tempter and chosen to sin. Sin arises because of bad choices. Every person is born into a life situation where choices need to be made. As infants we do not realize this. But as we grow older, we become aware of the freedom of choice and the need to take responsibility for our actions. We find ourselves in contexts which offer the potential for positive choices or for negative directions. We must live with our choices.

It was never different. Adam and Eve were placed into an environment in which there was the potential for good and for bad. They had to choose. The highly recommended choice was to stay in covenant relationship with God and to follow God's laws. To remain on the good way, they must worship God, not themselves or any object in the created order. Sin begins to invade human life when people break covenant with God and disobey God's laws. To take the wrong road and continue on it, is to embark upon the way of death.

The stage is set in the Garden of Eden (Genesis 2:8). The drama could move toward glory or it could disintegrate into shame. Everything humans need for life is there: trees to satisfy the thirst for beauty and trees enough to care for physical needs. Trees are symbolic of God's adequate provision for humankind. The challenge is to tend the garden with justice and compassion so that people are cared for and the created order flourishes.

The two trees in the midst of the garden—the tree of the knowledge of good and evil, and the tree of life—announce the choice that Adam and Eve—and we all—must make. God tells Adam not to eat of the fruit of knowledge. It will only lead to death (Genesis 2:17). Rather, drink wisdom from the true source, from God. Humans must choose.

Because of sin, all have fallen short of the Creator's intent, marred the image of God in which they were created, disrupted order in the world and limited their love for others. Adam and Eve made the wrong choice. Their act plunged the human race into a history of sin. The original event of sin and the fall (Genesis 3) has infested creation. As persons are born into the human race, they are born into a history and an environment which includes sinfulness (6:11–12). There is no getting around it. The tentacles of sin have extended themselves throughout time and they encircle every society and each individual.

There are many false alternatives. Throughout the centuries people have attached themselves to fake replacements of God: the worship of self, human philosophies, articles created by human hands, and many other temptations.

Sin is turning away from God and making gods of creation and of ourselves. We have only the bare outline of the story of the original sin of Adam and Eve. Yet it is clear what their sin was. They exchanged devotion to God's wisdom for devotion to their own knowledge. That is, they closed themselves off from the pathway of wisdom which God would reveal to them if they would remain in conversation (prayer) with God. Instead, they trusted their own minds. The result was the violation of their relationship with God.

To sin is to act against the commandments which were formed to uphold the covenant with God (Daniel 9:5). These commandments include right attitudes toward God and toward neighbour as well as respect for all creation. It is not possible to worship God with a clear conscience when God's commandments are not taken seriously and sin persists (Isaiah 1:12–17).

It is predictable—and evident—that once people make ultimate decisions based on their own self-invented values, they use these to rule over others and over creation. It is a small step from deciding who is right and who is wrong to deciding who lives and who dies. When we humans want to decide, on our own without reference to God, what is ultimately wise, we are on a collision course. To pit my truth against yours (in all seriousness) begins a spiral of violence whose end is self-destruction. Is the temptation to take life into our own hands implied in the desire to eat of the tree of life? (Genesis 3:22) Does God protect humankind from the impending self-destruction by guarding the way to the tree of life? (3:23–24) This is a gracious act of God!

Sin is violence. Sin as violence ranges all the way from breaking (violating) a promise or a relationship to doing physical violence against someone. According to the Bible, all sin, regardless toward whom it is directed, is the violation of the covenant relationship with God (Jeremiah 1:31–33).

Through sin, the powers of domination, division, destruction and death have been unleashed in humanity and in all of creation. Once sin enters a situation, it tends to take over. The biblical report of the temptation and fall of our first parents (Genesis 3) is followed by the story of Cain violating the life of his brother Abel (Genesis 4). Soon we hear of the wickedness of humankind in the time of Noah (Genesis 6) and the questionable project of building the Tower of Babel (Genesis 11).

Between these accounts we are told of how, again and again, God rescues the people from destruction. To protect them from further temptation, Adam and Eve were sent out of the garden. To protect him from retaliation, Cain was banned to the Land of Nod. Noah and his family were given protection in the ark. The people who schemed to build the tower to heaven, were prevented from following through with this foolish project when the Lord confused their languages, making it impossible to cooperate to the finish.

This is a rather discouraging performance on the part of the human race. But apparently it is a realistic portrayal. The more we sin, the more we become entrapped in sin. Once sin gains entrance into our individual and social lives, it infiltrates and eventually dominates. In time we find ourselves driven by the winds of evil.

The present-day recourse to violence in the family and in the community is a sign of the domination of sin. The fact that the great majority of the population in our lands craves violence in the entertainment and news media is a symptom and a generator of our enslavement to the power of sin. It seems hopeless even to attempt to stem the flow of violence. Does this describe our modern condition?

> Both Jews and Greeks are under the power of sin . . . . There is no one who is righteous . . . who has understanding, . . . who seeks God . . . who shows kindness . . . . Their feet are swift to shed blood; ruin and misery are in their paths, and the way of peace they have not known. There is no fear of God before their eyes (Romans 3:9–18).

Or this? "For all have sinned and fall short of the glory of God" (Romans 3:23). Has the condition even invaded the church, as it permeated "Jerusalem" in Daniel's day? "Jerusalem and your people have become a disgrace among all our neighbors" (Daniel 9:16).

The enslaving nature of sin is apparent in the powers of evil, which work through both individuals and groups and in the

entire created order. Jesus exposed the enslaving nature of sin. He saw it in a class of people called "sinners" (Luke 15:1), those disobedient to the law. But he also saw the enslavement of sin in those who thought they were spiritually clean, the "righteous" scribes and Pharisees (Matthew 23:27–28). Jesus was concerned not only with outward acts but with enslaving motivations such as lust (Matthew 5:27–30) and with deep-seated emotions such as anger (5:21–26). These manifestations of sin also show up in religious groups and in the church.

The power of evil pervades the structures of creation and the institutions of society. When the people of Israel wanted a king, the prophets warned that a system which relied on royalty could corrupt covenant faithfulness. And it did. Kings became rich at the expense of the poor. A "report card" on our environment gives today's consumer society an "F" for failure. We have polluted God's good creation with tons of garbage that will not decompose. We live in a world of nations that assumes the military right, under certain circumstances, to kill someone from another nation. We lose sight of the biblical conviction that violence is sin. How will God rescue us from ourselves?

> The Lord looks down from heaven on humankind to see if there are any who are wise and seek after God. They have all gone astray, they are all alike perverse; there is no one who does good, no, not one. Have they no knowledge, all are evildoers who eat up my people as they eat bread, and do not call upon the Lord? (Psalm 14:2–4)

But thanks be to God, who has not allowed the powers to reign supreme over creation or left humanity without hope. There is a solution to the problem depicted in this chapter. Through Jesus Christ, God has conquered sin and death and has called a people together to announce salvation to the world. What can we hope for and how shall we live in the face of sin and in the light of God's salvation?

> Do not let sin exercise dominion in your mortal bodies, to make you obey their passions. No longer present your members to sin as instruments of wickedness, but present yourselves to God as those who have been brought from death to life, and present your members to God as instruments of righteousness. For sin will have no dominion over you, since you are not under law but under grace (Romans 6:12–14).

And there is more we can do.

> Finally, be strong in the Lord and in the strength of his power. Put on the whole armor of God, so that you may be able to stand against the wiles of the devil. For our struggle is not against enemies of blood and flesh, but against the rulers, against the authorities, against the cosmic powers of this present darkness, against the spiritual forces of evil in the heavenly places (Ephesians 6:10–12).

Questions for Discussion

1. What is the root cause of sin? And why does sin continue among us?
2. What is the root definition of sin? What is the difference between sin and sins?
3. Give examples from history or from the present of how sin multiplies. Is this force inevitable or is it stoppable?
4. Sin is both individual and social. Give example of each, and discuss the difference between and the relationship of these two dimensions of sin.
5. Share experiences in which sin has been overcome in your life and/or in the life of acquaintances.

Salvation

With this chapter we come to the heart of the experiential side of the Christian faith. Christian faith is based on the belief that Jesus Christ is our Saviour, sent into the world as God's answer to the human quest for meaning and direction. The message of salvation in Jesus Christ is the most important foundation of the Christian faith. How shall we comprehend our salvation?

We believe that, through the life, death and resurrection of Jesus Christ, God offers salvation from sin and a new way of life to all people. To understand salvation, two things are required of us. First, we need to understand something of the meaning of salvation. This compels us to focus on Jesus Christ in the context of the biblical story of salvation. Second, we need to experience the meaning of salvation. This requires that we place ourselves within the biblical story of salvation and become part of it. Albert Schweitzer, the great doctor, missionary, theologian and organist, ended his book, *The Quest of the Historical Jesus,* with the words: ". . . as an ineffable mystery, they shall learn in their own experience Who He is."

From the beginning, God has acted with grace and mercy to bring about salvation. Our English word, *salvation,* is related to the notion of healing, as in the word *salve* (verb: to assuage; noun: ointment) and *to salvage* (to rescue). The German word for salvation, *Heil,* also carries the idea of "heal," as well as "whole" and "prosperous." This usage already suggests the rich cluster of meaning in our belief in salvation.

At the root of Old Testament terminology for salvation is the positive idea of broadening the space for something or someone so there is room to live and flourish. Thus one could envision a place of salvation as a land or a haven where there is sufficient food and protection for all to pursue abundant life.

Salvation is also the name for the rescue or deliverance that makes a safe life possible. A person is "saved" when rescued from any number of life-threatening situations: from military foes, from an angry attacker, from violence, from oppression, from drowning, from suffering, from disease, from blindness, from hopelessness, from a broken spirit, from false accusation, from selfishness, from hunger, from generational extinction, from chaos, or from the wrath to come. We see from this the intimate connection between salvation and peace (*shalom*), which also carries the meaning of wholeness.

Salvation is an event that saves people *from* something *for* something. For example, creation is a two-fold work of salvation, including: 1) deliverance *from* chaos, "a formless void and darkness" (Genesis 1:2) and, 2) the creation of a world designed *for* the flourishing of life (1:28). After the Fall, Adam and Eve needed salvation in two respects: 1) they needed to be rescued *from* the depths of sin, and 2) they needed positive guidance *for* a new beginning. In Psalm 40 the Psalmist recognizes this two-fold step of salvation: "He drew me up from the desolate pit, out of the miry bog, and set my feet upon a rock, making my steps secure" (Psalm 40:2). Jesus Christ saves us *from* spiritual death *for* discipleship.

The Bible is clear about the source of our salvation. Salvation is created and set in motion by God: "Salvation belongs to our God" (Revelation 7:10). The high point in Old Testament salvation history is God's act of saving the children of Israel from bondage in Egypt and bringing them to the promised land (Deuteronomy 6:20–25). In the New Testament salvation comes to focus and to fulfilment in and through Jesus Christ. "This Jesus . . . has become the cornerstone. There is salvation in no one else" (Acts 4:11–12).

In the fullness of time God sent his Son, whose faithfulness unto death on the cross has provided the way of salvation

for all people. The Bible is emphatic about the universality of the invitation to salvation. All are invited. This is already promised in the call of Abraham to generate a chosen people (Genesis 12:1–3). The New Testament brings this news especially to Gentiles and others who had felt themselves shut out from God's salvation because of the seemingly exclusive emphasis on the people of Israel. Many were overjoyed to hear that they too had a share in the mercy of the Lord.

Jesus' pilgrimage to the cross tells the world that his death is for all people. He made his way open-handedly. He did not take sides. When he was abused, he did not return abuse (1 Peter 2:23). He spoke words of forgiveness to Jews and Romans. In this he showed that his death was for everyone. If he had done otherwise, we could not say: "God so loved the world . . ." (John 3:16).

By his death and resurrection, he breaks the powers of sin and death, cancels our debt of sin and opens the way to new life. Theories of salvation have been developed by theologians over the years. These can be summarized into three main groups: the Victor theory, the Substitution theory and the Example theory. Each theory relies on selected verses from the Bible. Let us look briefly at each of these.

The "Christ the Victor" theory, developed by early church leaders, builds on the teaching that Christ was victorious over the power of evil that enslaved us because of Adam's sin. Christ took on human flesh "so that through death he might destroy the one who has the power of death, that is, the devil, and free those who all their lives were held in slavery by the fear of death" (Hebrews 2:14–15).

The Substitution theory says that Christ died on the cross as a substitute for us. To atone for Adam's sin (and our sins) we should die. But God sent Jesus to die in our place. This truth is expressed in the following text: "They are now justified by his grace as a gift, through the redemption that is in Christ Jesus, whom God put forward as a sacrifice of atonement by his blood, effective through faith" (Romans 3:24–25).

The "Christ the Example" theory points to the death of Christ as a demonstration of God's love for us. We are drawn to God by the example of his son. The apostle Paul writes to the Romans: "God proves his love for us in that while we still were sinners Christ died for us" (Romans 5:8). The late Mennonite theologian, John C. Wenger, identified this theory as closest to a Mennonite understanding of salvation. At the same time he held, as we should, that we need not attach ourselves to any one of the theories. Let our understanding of salvation be nurtured by the great biblical texts that focus on God's salvation for us.

Mennonites have taken special note of the connection made in the Scriptures between the cross of Christ and our cross. This is seen in passages such as the following: "When you were dead in trespasses . . . God made you alive together with him" (Colossians 2:13). "We have been buried with him by baptism into death . . . so we too might walk in newness of life" (Romans 6:4). We have been "saved by grace through faith" so that we might continue the works of salvation which God desires of us (Ephesians 2:8–9).

The meeting between Jesus and Zacchaeus, the tax collector, illustrates the close connection between Christ's salvation and our response (Luke 19:1–10). At the end of their meeting, Zacchaeus confesses his sins by announcing that he will share half his wealth with the poor. On the basis of Zacchaeus' commitment, which includes a transformation of heart and a step of obedience, Jesus says: "Today salvation has come to this house . . . for the Son of Man came to seek out and to save the lost" (19:9–10). Here justification and justice, two aspects of salvation, work hand in hand.

When we hear the good news of the love of God, the Holy Spirit moves us to accept the gift of salvation. The Christian experience of salvation is ongoing. This comes to light in the

The new birth consists, verily,
  not in water nor in words; but
it is the heavenly, living, and quickening
    power of God in our hearts
    which flows forth from God, and which
    by the preaching of the divine Word,
    if we accept it by faith,
    quickens, renews, pierces, and
    converts our hearts,
so that we are changed and converted
    from unbelief to faith,
    from unrighteousness to righteousness,
    from evil to good,
    from carnality to spirituality,
    from the earthly to the heavenly,
    from the wicked nature of Adam
    to the good nature of Jesus Christ.
                                    —Menno Simons

New Testament's references to "new birth" (John 3:3; 1 Peter
1:3; 1 John 3:9; 4:7; 5:1–3). The Bible uses this term to cover
the entire lifespan of Christian experience. The imagery of new
birth points not only to the *initial step* of becoming a Christian,
but to the *ongoing experience* of salvation, as well as the
ultimate experience of resurrection from death.

Jesus speaks to Nicodemus of the *initial step* (John 3). It is
not enough to be born into a Jewish family and tradition. You
must be born a second time, "from above" (v.3), "of the Spirit"
(v.9). The first is our physical birth; the second our spiritual
rebirth. Whether in a remembered moment or gradually over
time, it is necessary for persons who call themselves Christian
believers to embrace the gift of salvation personally.

Salvation as an *ongoing experience* of new birth is a theme
in 1 John. "Those who have been born of God do not sin
because God's seed abides in them" (3:9). The new birth is
expressed in their obedience to God's commandments, including love for one another (4:7; 5:1–3). The emphasis in 1 John
reminds us of Menno Simons who depicted the ongoing
salvation experience as "walking in the resurrection."

Jesus' resurrection from death was the *ultimate experience*
in his accomplishment of salvation. Our resurrection from death
will be the ultimate experience of our salvation, ushering us
into eternal life. God "has given us a new birth into a living
hope through the resurrection of Jesus Christ from the dead" (1
Peter 1:3). We anticipate our resurrection as a future experience
of new birth.

**We believe that the salvation we have already experienced
is but a foretaste of the salvation yet to come**. In the Book of
Revelation the cry of the multitude, "Salvation belongs to our
God who sits upon the throne, and to the Lamb" (Revelation
7:10), is not only a cry of thanksgiving for sins forgiven, but
also, and much more, a sign of the coming salvation in the form
of "a new heaven and a new earth" (21:1). Here salvation

includes the fulfilment of God's promise for creation.

Meanwhile, says the apostle Paul, "all of us, with unveiled faces, seeing the glory of the Lord as though reflected in a mirror, are being transformed into the same image from one degree of glory to another; for this comes from the Lord, the Spirit" (2 Corinthians 3:18).

Questions for Discussion

1. What is the problem for which salvation is the solution?
2. Identify insights from the Old Testament that are important for an understanding of salvation.
3. How do the life, death, resurrection and second coming of Christ relate to our salvation.
4. Share personal experiences of salvation.
5. How will salvation be a future experience?

The Church of Jesus Christ

The birth of the church was God's creation. God had in mind to organize a community of people committed to the Lord. Through this people God would reveal grace and accomplish purposes. God's chosen people would provide a special channel for salvation. This is a high and holy beginning which doesn't always fit the reality of the church today. But it should tell us something about the aspiration God has for the church. It is important that we begin our thinking about the church with a confession of what we believe the church should be and become.

We believe that the church is the assembly of those who have accepted God's offer of salvation through faith in Jesus Christ. The formation of a special community called the people of God has its background in Egypt when the Israelites were slaves in that country. This was a time of suffering, a time of yearning for freedom. In that setting, God said to the Israelites: "I will take you as my people, and I will be your God. You shall know that I am the Lord your God, who has freed you from the burdens of the Egyptians" (Exodus 6:7). It is of great importance to note that God works in and through community (the people of God) to accomplish salvation.

One thing led to the next. Under God's miraculous protection, the people embarked on a journey which eventually brought them to the promised land. There they developed a livelihood and built up a community with its institutions and tribes. While their story includes both faithfulness and unfaithfulness, they continued to affirm God as their originator and the guarantor of their destiny: "And you established your people Israel for yourself to be your people forever; and you, O Lord, became their God" (2 Samuel 7:24). The Israelite people of God were a special people in God's plan, the chosen race.

Chosen for what? Abraham and Sarah had been promised that their descendants would provide a blessing to all peoples of the earth. This blessing was the Messiah, Jesus Christ. Jesus would again become the firstborn of a re-created people of God. This renewed people was not limited biologically to those of Abraham's seed. All peoples of the earth were welcome to join. The only provision was that they should confess Jesus Christ as the Son of God in word and in deed.

The church began as a people comprised of many nations of the world. This was evident on Pentecost Day when the cultural and religious walls surrounding the people of Israel were suddenly breaking down. Now the invitation is open for anyone to join the people. A new "nation" was coming to birth:

> But you are a chosen race, a royal priesthood, a holy nation, God's own people, in order that you may proclaim the mighty acts of him who called you out of darkness into his marvellous light. Once you were not a people, but now you are God's people; once you had not received mercy, but now you have received mercy (1 Peter 2:9–10).

The church is Christ's church. He is its sponsor and its instructor. He is its guarantor, since he said: "I will build my church, and the gates of Hades (or Hell) will not prevail against it" (Matthew 16:18). We read that "Christ loved the church and gave himself up for her" (Ephesians 5:5). Jesus Christ has invested much in the church. That is why Christians should take the church seriously.

We acknowledge the church as the society of believers from many nations, anointed for witness by the Holy Spirit. Do you find yourself stumbling over the description of the church as a "society?" Some Christians think of the church as existing somewhere in the clouds, as a perfect spiritual idea. Others want the church to be locked within the heart of the individual. But the church is real people meeting together in associations, as societies. The church is not just any social gathering. Its basis is different from any other: "For no one can lay any foundation other than the one that has been laid; that foundation is Jesus Christ" (1 Corinthians 3:11).

The society of believers is multi-national, an ethnic mosaic. It breaks open the ethnic groups we are tempted to form. Even if we are in a congregation where the people are mostly of one ethnic background, the worldwide church is larger and much more diverse. "For in the one Spirit we were all baptized into one body—Jews or Greeks, slave or free—and we were all made to drink of one Spirit" (1 Corinthians 12:12–13).

The kingdom of God always extends itself beyond political borders. "But you will receive power when the Holy Spirit has come upon you; and you will be my witnesses in Jerusalem, in Judea and Samaria, and to the ends of the earth" (Acts 1:8). The church's mission is international in scope and vision.

It took an earthshaking event to get the church moving into the future of its history. The event happened in Jerusalem after the ascension of Jesus to heaven. It was the day of Pentecost, the Hebrew thanksgiving festival. There were some miraculous manifestations of power (Acts 2:1–11). With that the Holy Spirit entered the place where the disciples were gathered with people from various countries. A miracle happened through which everyone heard the good news about Jesus Christ in their own language.

At first the people were puzzled about this miracle: "How is it that we hear, each of us in our own native language?" (Acts 2:8). The apostle Peter quoted from the prophet Joel: "In the last days it will be, God declares, that I will pour out my Spirit on *all* flesh" (2:17). Some time later the believers could praise God and say: "Then God has given even to the Gentiles the repentance that leads to life" (11:18). God was telling them, through the power of the Holy Spirit, that what Jesus said and did is not only for Old Testament people but for everyone. That's why the church has an open door today. That's why you and I are welcome among the people of God.

The church is the assembly of those who voluntarily commit themselves to follow Christ in life and to be accountable to one another and to God. The Mennonite church is a "believers church." This means you first make the decision to believe in Christ, then you become a member through baptism and public acceptance. Being born into a Christian family or into a Christian country does not make you a member of the Christian faith or the Christian church. You need to decide this voluntarily.

Voluntary participation was introduced on the day of Pentecost. The disciple Peter preached a message and gave the open invitation. Then "those who welcomed his message were baptized" (Acts 2:41). Through the centuries this emphasis became blurred, especially with the introduction of infant baptism. The Anabaptists of the sixteenth century helped restore the idea of voluntary membership. At that time, being a Christian had become confused with being born into a so-called "Christian country."

The early church had a simple way of being the church: "They devoted themselves to the apostles' teaching and fellowship, to the breaking of bread and the prayers" (Acts 2:42). They also cared for each other economically. At least in the earliest years, they shared their goods "and had all things in common" (2:44).

The church is the household, or family, of God. Jesus had a way of cutting through the formalities to the core of life as it should be. Thus when some critics told him he was neglecting his family responsibilities, he took the occasion to emphasize that all are brothers and sisters one of another. It does not depend on the bloodline. "He replied: 'Who are my mother and my brothers?' And looking at those who sat around him, he said, 'Here are my mother and my brothers! Whoever does the will of God is my brother and sister and mother'" (Mark 3:33–35).

This sets the stage for our understanding of the church as a spiritual family. All are sisters and brothers in the church. All in the church, regardless of age, are children of God. All of us are adopted sons and daughters of God. I remember my older brother coming to me on the Sunday of my baptism. He shook my hand and said: "Welcome, brother, into the church!" Now I was a "brother" to him in a new way.

Let's not be a closed family. The Bible reminds us to open our doors and hearts to all people: "You shall also love the stranger, for you were strangers in the land of Egypt" (Deuteronomy 10:19). "Contribute to the needs of the saints; extend hospitality to strangers" (Romans 12:13). Hospitality and inclusiveness go hand in hand. The Letter to the Ephesians encourages Gentile believers who feel excluded: "So then, you are no longer strangers and aliens, but you are citizens with the saints and also members of the household of God" (Ephesians 2:19).

We believe that the church as the body of Christ is the visible manifestation of Jesus Christ. The church is the body of Christ. Members of the church are members of his body. What does the body do? It does what Jesus did when he was in his body on earth. He healed the sick. He taught people the wisdom of God. He called upon people to love one another. He invited people to follow God's ways. He helped people fallen by the wayside. He supported the "losers" in society. He spoke the truth even when it was difficult to do so. He preferred to suffer rather than cause suffering.

The Bible is rich in body language when it describes life in community. Here is one example: "We must grow up in every way into him who is the head, into Christ, from whom the whole body, joined and knit together by every ligament with which it is equipped, as each part is working properly, promotes the body's growth in building itself up in love" (Ephesians 4:15–16).

The church exists as a community of believers in the local congregation, as a community of congregations and as the worldwide community of faith. All believers who acknowledge Jesus Christ as Saviour and Lord are members of his body, the church. This includes people around the world. There is one universal church, embracing all congregations, conferences and denominations everywhere.

Wherever God's people meet regularly to devote themselves to worship, prayer, teaching the Scriptures, observing baptism and communion, caring for one another and serving to extend the gospel through mission and service, there is the local expression of the true church.

> Now to him who by the power at work within us is able to accomplish abundantly far more than all we can ask or imagine, to him be glory in the church and in Christ Jesus to all generations, forever and ever. Amen (Ephesians 3:20–21).

Questions for Discussion

1. Read 1 Corinthians 12, Romans 12, 1 Peter 2. Reflect on the images of the church used in these passages. What other metaphors are used in the Bible?
2. Why was the international character of the church of great importance in New Testament times? Why is this aspect important even today?
3. How important is accountability to one another? Is it easy or is it difficult to be accountable to others in the church?
4. How is the church like a family? How is the church not like a family?
5. Have you experienced or observed repentance and conversion in the life of people in the church? Where and how?

The Church in Mission

Jesus came to earth for a purpose. His task was to accomplish an assignment given to him by God, and to give an assignment to his followers before his departure. His assignment from God had two parts: to take upon himself the sins of the world, and to leave us the example of a life lived according to the will of God. His assignment to his followers also had two parts: to tell others the good news about forgiveness of sins, and to follow Jesus' pathway of life in our day. This assignment can be summed up in the word "mission." What do we believe about the Christian mission?

We believe that the church is called to proclaim and to be a sign of the kingdom of God. We have an instrument through which we can carry out Jesus' commission to us. The instrument is the church, the body of believers. Through this body, the church, Jesus commissions us to continue the mission he began while on earth.

The church carries out God's mission by doing and by being. *Doing* includes a variety of activities, such as proclaiming Jesus as Saviour of humankind, announcing God's forgiveness of sinners, healing diseases, inviting persons of all backgrounds to enjoy God's love and preaching justice for the oppressed. *Being* means being a sign of God's presence in the world. A faithful community in which there is love for one another and in which God's praises are sung and God's word is preached becomes a sign pointing to God. Our mission is to be the church.

What does the mission of the church have to do with the kingdom of God? When Jesus spoke of the kingdom, he meant the reign of God. He was not thinking of one specific country as God's kingdom. The kingdom of God is a spiritual reality that encompasses the earth. God's reign is present wherever God's will is done in the hearts and lives of people, in their relationships to and in all dimensions of the created order. This happens in countless ways and places at any given moment.

There were right and wrong understandings of the kingdom of God among the people of the Old Testament. At times they thought of the kingdom of God as bounded by their little land just east of the Mediterranean Sea. Yet the prophets envisioned the entire earth as God's domain. At times the people thought only Israelites belonged to the kingdom of God. Yet the prophets saw all people of the earth as potential citizens of God's kingdom. At times the people thought the kingdom was a land to be defended with military might. The prophets called upon the people to melt their military weapons into farming tools: "beat their swords into ploughshares and their spears into pruning hooks" (Isaiah 2:4). Today we face the same temptations and need to hear the same message about God's kingdom.

In his mission of preaching, teaching and healing, Jesus announced, "The kingdom of God has come near; repent, and believe in the good news." Signs of God's kingdom were already evident in Old Testament times. There was repentance. There was forgiveness. There was healing. There were acts of justice—people were sharing their bread with the poor. And there was a community, the people of God, a sign of the kingdom upon earth.

Yet there was a persistent expectation of more to come. The spiritually sensitive leaders in Israel lived by promises. Abraham and Sarah received the promise that their descendants would bring blessing to all people. Their son Isaac and their grandson Jacob received and believed the same promise. Moses was shown the promised land where the people of Abraham could flourish as a nation.

Later the prophets of Israel spoke of something greater and

better than a promised land and a national identity. Their hope was focused in the promise of a Messiah who would be there for all people. His reign would break down barriers of land and nationhood. The promised one would clarify the mission of God and would gather a committed people from all nations and from all walks of life.

Jesus came with the announcement of God's mission: "The time is fulfilled, and the kingdom of God has come near; repent, and believe in the good news"(Mark 1:15). He helped the Jews to understand the will of God for their people. And he surprised many by broadening their horizon to think of God's reign among all peoples of the earth and in lands beyond Judea.

Some time after Jesus left the earth, one of his disciples, Peter, summarized this broadened mission in a sermon: "You know the message God sent to the people of Israel, preaching peace by Jesus Christ—he is Lord of all" (Acts 10:36). It is the church's mission to proclaim this message, that Christ is Lord of all, and to do so by preaching peace.

The church is called to witness to the reign of Christ by embodying Jesus' way in its own life and patterning itself after the reign of God. It's not an easy assignment to embody the way of Jesus in our day. It requires that we begin with a vision of how things could be. This means we may need to take the road less travelled. The majority of people on earth do not believe that, in practice, you should turn the other cheek, as Jesus taught. Sharing of our abundance with those who have little does not come naturally to people. It is not easy to go out of your way to help the hurting person. It is not popular to be a conscientious objector to war when the government is calling young people to fight for their country. But this is what it means to follow Jesus' way. Deep joy and lasting satisfaction fill the hearts of those who travel this road.

The church is also to give witness by proclaiming the reign of God in word and deed. We express ourselves through actions and with words. The two go hand in hand. Words support actions and actions back up words. We speak through our actions, and we act through our words. There is an intimate connection between word and deed. Jesus fulfilled God's mission using both actions and words. He healed the sick (Matthew 4:23–24); he taught the people (Matthew 5–7). In this way the kingdom of God came near to the people (10:9).

He also commissioned his hearers to act and to speak. They were to sell, to give, to follow (Mark 10:21) and to teach (Matthew 28:20). He sent seventy disciples out with the words: "Whenever you enter a town . . . cure the sick who are there, and say to them, 'The kingdom of God has come near to you'" (Luke 10:9). Deeds ("cure the sick") and words ("say to them") are the medium of the Christian message. In both ways we have opportunity to "tell of God's salvation from day to day" (1 Chronicles 16:23).

In its programs, the Mennonite church expresses its mission in these two dimensions. Among us we find some institutions which lean in the one direction and some in the other. Mennonite Central Committee emphasizes deeds. Our mission boards emphasize proclamation in word, through preaching, through teaching, through personal evangelism, and in other ways.

Such witness is a response to Jesus' call to make disciples. Jesus said to his disciples: "As the Father has sent me, so I send you"(John 20:21). Over the past century or more the Mennonite churches of Europe and North America have sent many missionaries across the seas to Africa, Asia and South America. The result is that today Christian congregations with Mennonite connections can be found in 75 or more countries of the world.

In the past several decades Mennonite churches in countries where Mennonites have lived for many years have begun to open their doors to persons of diverse ethnic backgrounds. As a result, in Paraguay, in Canada and in the United States there are Mennonite congregations of aboriginal peoples. Additionally, in North America there are congregations where the gospel is preached in such languages as Chinese, Taiwanese, Japanese, Spanish, French, Laotian and Hmong. Like the first Pentecost of Acts 2, we are experiencing a "miracle of tongues."

It is significant that persons are attracted to the Mennonite church because of its proclamation of the message of peace and justice. The good news Jesus brought included the call for people and nations to live in peace here and now (Luke 2:14). His teachings included good news for the poor and the hungry, for the imprisoned and those who were excluded from community. Jesus expected of his followers that they would bring God's justice to such persons. The church which proclaims and works for peace and justice is the church in mission.

God calls the church to direct its mission to people from all nations and ethnic backgrounds. Jesus lived in a society where racial sensitivities were tense. Which nation you belonged to and which race you were part of mattered greatly. Religious convictions were usually tied in with racial identity. Jesus made it clear that he did not take sides. He ministered to everyone, whether Jew or Gentile. Also, he did not distinguish between rich or poor, male or female, child or adult, sinner or saint. He lived for all, and he died and rose for all.

This universal emphasis shines through in his words to Nicodemus: "For God so loved *the world* that he gave his only Son, so that *everyone* who believes in him should not perish, but have eternal life"(John 3:16) (italics mine). We find this same emphasis in Jesus' parting words to the disciples when he sends them to witness "in Jerusalem, in all Judea and Samaria, and to the ends of the earth" (Acts 1:8).

Questions for Discussion

1. According to the teaching and example of Jesus, what is the mission of the church?
2. Why is mission a part of the life of the church?

3. Can the mission of the church be carried out, at least in part, by simply "being" a faithful community of Christians.
4. Mennonites emphasize the importance of witness not only in word but also in deed. How can these be held together? How and where are you involved in mission?

Baptism

On the worldwide Christian scene, the Mennonite way of baptizing puts them in a minority. The majority of Christian churches practice pedobaptism (infant baptism) while Mennonites practice what is called adult baptism or believers baptism. This means: first believe, then be baptized. Persons are baptized following their personal statement of faith and commitment to Christ and his body, the church.

Churches that practice pedobaptism do so based on the sheer grace of God and a prayerful hope that the infant will own and confirm the faith at a later time. The commitment of parents and church are important in the act. It is not for us to judge the practice of infant baptism. Today, in a spirit of Christian grace, there is a growing respect for differing practices of other denominations. At the same time, believers baptism is a distinguishing mark of the Mennonite church, with a strong conviction about its biblical and theological appropriateness.

We believe that the baptism of believers with water is a sign of their cleansing from sin. The Mennonite conviction about baptism goes back to the Anabaptist movement at the time of the Protestant Reformation in the sixteenth century. The setting was Zurich, Switzerland. A young adult by the name of Conrad Grebel and some friends concluded, on the basis of Bible study, that infant baptism did not have a biblical foundation. They made their views known and promptly got themselves into trouble with authorities of the church and of the government. This led to a public debate on January 17, 1525, which resulted in a court decision to uphold infant baptism. Grebel and his friends were told to cease their Bible studies.

This did not stop the movement. Soon after at a Bible study meeting, Grebel baptized Georg Blaurock, who in turn baptized others in the group. This baptismal event is of great significance in church history. It marked a break with the state church and the beginning of the free church movement. "Free church" means people become Christians and members of the church by voluntary (free) choice, not by natural birth into a biological family and citizenship in a country. These radical young people gained the nickname "anabaptist" (re-baptizers).

About this time a priest in Holland by the name of Menno Simons (1496–1561) heard about persons being put to death for baptizing adults rather than children. At first he was puzzled by these radicals. He began to search the Scriptures and, to his surprise, could find no basis for infant baptism. He concluded that the Bible teaches that God takes care of little children regardless of any ritual that is performed upon them. Menno became convinced that adult baptism was the right way. Because of his convictions, Menno was pursued as a heretic. Yet he was joyful in the Lord.

Today many church groups practice believers baptism and some, who were formerly convinced of infant baptism only, are reconsidering their stance and opening the way for adult baptism as well.

Baptism is a pledge before the church of a believer's covenant with God to walk in the way of Jesus Christ through the power of the Holy Spirit. Most churches practising adult baptism put the emphasis on baptism being an individual testimony of the acceptance of salvation in Christ. The Mennonite approach certainly includes this but adds another important dimension. Baptism goes together with membership in the church. A public commitment to Jesus Christ goes hand in hand with attachment to the church, the body of Christ. Living out one's Christian obedience and maturing in faith and life are not individual matters. We give ourselves to God in and through the community of believers.

Why connect baptism with church membership? When John

the Baptist appeared on the banks of the River Jordan, he called upon people to repent and be baptized. He stood at the very place where centuries before the people of Israel had entered the Promised Land after their escape from Egypt and their trek through the wilderness. Just before entering the land, they had made a solemn promise to be a holy people, a faithful community, unto the Lord. However, things had not developed as they had promised.

Thus John the Baptist issued a call for repentance and for a renewed commitment to become a community under God. Baptism ("going through the Jordan River") was a symbolic way of re-entering the community with renewed commitment to God. It became evident to the people who gathered around John that the new community of which he spoke was about to welcome a new leader, Jesus. When Jesus appeared on the horizon, John pointed to him as the new Messiah who would baptize with the Holy Spirit all those who would join this company of the committed.

The use of water to symbolize religious meaning has a long-standing tradition in the Scriptures. The flood waters cleansed the earth of wickedness in Noah's day. The waters of the Red Sea and of the Jordan River prepared Israel to be God's special people. In a sense, these were regarded as group baptisms. The prophet Isaiah referred to water as a medium for cleansing the people from their sins (Isaiah 1:16). Priests and people engaged in ritual washings to prepare for worship. Gentiles who wished to join the Jewish faith needed to undergo proselyte baptism to do so. Given its importance in life, it is understandable that water easily becomes a symbol for spiritual realities.

Against this background, we can see that the form of baptism is not an issue. If the activity involving water is meant to symbolize cleansing, at least three forms suggest themselves. At times we wash ourselves by submerging totally. At times we sprinkle water on face and hands and body, as when showering. At other times we pour water over the area that needs cleansing.

So too Christian baptism has utilized all three modes of cleansing for baptism.

Some denominations still argue over which is the right form. But happily this is not an issue as it once was. It is best if a congregation, and even a denomination, adopts one standard form of baptism. Then no one in the church is tempted to pretend to be holier than the rest because of the form of baptism. For the rest, we should respect the different forms in use in the wider Christian church.

Believers are baptized into Christ and his body by the Spirit, water and blood. The Bible names three signs that point us in the right direction in Christian life. "There are three that testify: the Spirit and the water and the blood, and these three agree" (1 John 5:7–8). Water, Spirit and blood remind us of key aspects of a life committed to Jesus Christ. All three are connected with baptism. Each speaks of a dimension of the meaning of baptism.

Baptism with *water* is a sign of cleansing from sin. At Pentecost people heard Peter's message and asked, "What shall we do?" Peter said to them, "Repent and be baptized every one of you in the name of Jesus Christ so that your sins may be forgiven" (Acts 2:38). The water used in baptisms today symbolizes and supports our personal testimony that we have repented of sins and we accept the forgiveness God offers us. Just as water washes away dirt and refreshes our bodies, so baptismal water points to the cleansing and refreshing we experience when touched by God. This ritual done in the company of believers signals our commitment to live as repentant and forgiven people.

Baptism with the *Holy Spirit* is a sign of the renewing and quickening power of God in the believer's life. At Jesus' baptism the Spirit appeared as a dove descending on him (Mark 1:10; see also John 1:33). At Pentecost the gift of the Holy Spirit was promised to those who were baptized (Acts

2:38–39). On that occasion the Spirit was evident in the dramatic open-heartedness with which the first believers accepted people of many nations. The Spirit was also active in bringing assurance to the believers that their faith was on the right track.

The baptism of *blood* is a reference to a commitment to faithfulness, even unto suffering and death. Jesus referred to his suffering and death when he said: "I have a baptism with which to be baptized, and what stress I am under until it is completed!"(Luke 12:50). On one occasion Jesus challenged his disciples: "You do not know what you are asking. Are you able to drink the cup that I drink, or be baptized with the baptism that I am baptized with?"(Mark 10:38).

Our commitment to Jesus' way brings with it the same prospect of the baptism of suffering and death. We can understand this to mean that when we face suffering and death faithfully, whether because of natural causes or because of convictions to which we hold, these experiences in the course of life and at the end of life are part of Christian baptism. The Anabaptists spoke of their persecution and suffering as a baptism of blood.

Seen in this three-fold way, we understand why even Jesus was baptized. First, in doing so he identified with the new community committed to the new covenant. Second, his baptism was the occasion for the revelation that the Holy Spirit is available in a special way through the Son of God (Mark 1:10). Third, his baptism was a sign of his commitment to a baptism of blood. His was a baptism unto death.

Christian baptism is for those who confess their sins, repent, accept Jesus Christ as Saviour and Lord, and commit themselves to follow Christ in obedience as members of his body. Baptism has no magical power. It does not make a person different. It gives no automatic assurance of salvation. A baptismal service proclaims a message about how

God regards people who have faith. For the person being baptized, baptism signifies a personal commitment.

> Should we continue in sin in order that grace may abound? By no means! How can we who died to sin go on living in it? Do you not know that all of us who have been baptized into Christ Jesus were baptized into his death? Therefore we have been buried with him by baptism into death, so that, just as Christ was raised from the dead by the glory of the Father, so we too might walk in newness of life (Romans 6:1–4).

Baptism marks a choice. The water of baptism soon disappears, but the remembrance of the public testimony in the presence of the congregation remains. I recall my baptism often. It marked a decision in my life. From that time forward I knew I should take Christ and the church seriously in what I say and do. To be baptized into Christ means to incorporate Christ's life into one's very being. "As many of you as were baptized into Christ have clothed yourselves with Christ" (Galatians 3:27). My baptism was a testimony of my commitment to Jesus Christ and to the church.

Questions for Discussion

1. Baptism is a distinguishing mark of what it means to belong to the church. How do Mennonites understand baptism, and why?
2. Who should be invited to be baptized?
3. Why are baptism and church membership closely linked in Mennonite theology? What is the biblical basis?
4. Baptism involves more than water. What is the meaning of Spirit baptism and of baptism of blood?
5. What is the choice that baptism marks? If you have not been baptized, how could baptism make a difference in your life? If you are baptized, how has it made a difference?

The Lord's Supper

Three or more times a year, baptized members of the congregation do something that could appear strange to someone looking in from the outside. In the context of solemn worship they eat a small morsel of bread and drink a small quantity of grape juice or wine. This is called a supper, the Lord's Supper. What is the meaning of this practice?

We believe that the Lord's Supper is a sign by which the church thankfully remembers the new covenant which Jesus established by his death. The Lord's Supper is a meal of remembrance. Shortly before Jesus went to the cross, the Hebrew people celebrated the Passover meal. This was done to remember the escape from Egypt, particularly the night when the angel of death "passed over" the families of the Israelites on its way to the homes of the Egyptians. Jesus called his disciples together for this meal as well.

At the table, Jesus told of his impending death. He then instructed his disciples to remember his shed blood and his broken body every time they celebrate this occasion (Luke 22:15–20). With these instructions from our Lord, the Passover meal of the Old Testament becomes the Lord's Supper of the New Testament. Just as the first Lord's Supper pointed to the death of Jesus, which would happen in only a few more days, so the continuing celebration of the Lord's Supper points back, as a sign, to the death of Christ. As we eat and drink, we remember that Christ died for us.

Not all church groups interpret the Lord's Supper in such a simple and straightforward way: as a sign and a reminder. Some Christian churches take the event in other directions. Roman Catholics regard the meal as a sacrament. Many believe the bread and wine (the elements) actually become the flesh and blood of Christ. The word for this change is *transubstantiation*. Lutheran churches regard the meal as a symbol. Luther emphasized that the real presence of Christ is in the elements, even though the elements themselves remain bread and wine. The word for this symbolic presence is *consubstantiation*.

Mennonites, like some of their Anabaptist forebears, prefer to speak of the Lord's Supper as a meal of remembrance and a sign. This follows the simple and straightforward interpretation and instruction of Christ, stated in Paul's letter to the church at Corinth: "And when he had given thanks, he broke it [the loaf of bread] and said: 'This is my body that is for you. Do this in remembrance of me.' In the same way he took the cup also, after supper, saying, 'This cup is the new covenant in my blood. Do this, as often as you drink it, in remembrance of me'"(1 Corinthians 11:24–25)

The Lord's Supper points to Jesus Christ, whose body was given for us and whose shed blood established the new covenant. The Lord's Supper is a covenant meal. During the institution of the Lord's Supper, Jesus said: "This is my blood of the covenant, which is poured out for many for the forgiveness of sins" (Matthew 26:28). In what way is the Lord's Supper a covenant?

The Lord's Supper was and is the event marking the sign(ing) of a new covenant. Here "sign(ing)" is meant in three ways. The Lord's Supper is sign-language (as among the deaf) of the event it proclaims, the death of Christ. The Lord's Supper is a road sign, pointing Christian pilgrims to the origin of their journey (the cross of Christ) and to their destination (the return of Christ). The Lord's Supper is the occasion when, in a manner of speaking, God signs a new covenant (contract) with the people of God.

The old covenant, made with the patriarchs, promised a Saviour. The new covenant proclaims that the Saviour has come and a new era has begun. With this, the Scripture from Jeremiah has been fulfilled:

> But this is the covenant that I will make with the house of Israel after those days, says the Lord: I will put my law within them, and I will write it on their hearts; and I will be their God, and they shall be my people. No longer shall they teach one another, or say to each other, "Know the Lord," for they shall all know me, from the least of them to the greatest, says the Lord; for I will forgive their iniquity, and remember their sin no more (Jeremiah 31:33–34).

The supper re-presents the presence of the risen Christ in the church. The Lord's Supper is a time for renewal. You haven't seen a friend for some time. She comes to town. You arrange to have lunch together. There's hardly enough time to catch up on everything that has happened. But you are satisfied that you have connected again. You feel you know each other in a new way. It was a good time to update the relationship—all because you re-connected. The reconnection involved more than simply establishing old ties. New experiences call for rearrangements of relationships. You aren't the same people you once were. You have renewed your relationship.

Our relationship with Christ benefits from periodic renewal as we change and mature. Spiritual growth takes place on the edge of meaningful encounter with the risen Christ. In calling to mind the death of Christ, the event is drawn forward in time. The drama of the Lord's Supper helps that to happen. We experience renewal in the inner person and in our relationships to God and to one another. The grace of Christ overwhelms us anew. The love of Christ draws us to himself. We renew our acquaintance with the Lord.

Spiritual renewal happens in two specific ways in relation to the bread and the cup. This is indicated in the words of the apostle Paul to the Corinthians: "The cup of blessing that we bless, is it not a sharing [koinonia or fellowship] in the blood of

Christ? The bread that we break, is it not a sharing [koinonia or fellowship] in the body of Christ? Because there is one bread, we who are many are one body, for we all partake of the one bread" (1 Corinthians 10:16–17).

The *cup* re-presents the suffering and death of Christ. When Jesus wrestled with death in Gethsemane, he prayed: "Father, if you are willing, remove this cup from me" (Luke 22:42). The contents of the cup re-present the life given up by the shedding of blood. When we drink of the cup, we share in the blessing of Christ's death. This sharing includes the benefit of the atonement he made for sins and the benefit of the comfort Christ gives in our times of suffering because of the crosses we carry.

The *bread* brings to remembrance the privilege and responsibility of being his body, the church. We are one with all faithful people of God from the beginning of time until now.

Remembering how Jesus laid down his life for his friends, we his followers recommit ourselves to the way of the cross. The Lord's Supper is an act of commitment. We remember how after the first Lord's Supper Jesus spoke to his disciples about finding true greatness in servanthood (Luke 22:24–30). We remember how he challenged his followers to follow all the way to the cross (22:31–46). We remember how they forsook him and he proceeded on alone, laying down his life for them and for everyone in the world. We remember; we repent; we recommit ourselves to the way of the cross.

Food is a source of energy and strength. It gives momentum and endurance to physical life. In the same way, spiritual food strengthens our faith and the inner person. In eating and drinking the elements together with others and with a keen sense of spiritual nearness to our Lord, we are nourished for Christian pilgrimage.

Invited to the Lord's table are all who have been baptized into the community of faith, who are living at peace with their brothers and sisters in the faith, and who are willing

to be accountable in their congregation. The Lord's Supper affirms and promotes Christian unity. The apostle Paul chides the church at Corinth for the disunity and for allowing individualism to flourish among them. They eat the Lord's Supper, but it has no meaning since there are divisions among them and since they eat in a disorderly way. They look out only for themselves and disregard others (1 Corinthians 11:17–22). Where unity is missing, the meal is not the Lord's Supper. Where brothers and sisters are not accountable to one another, the Lord's Supper is a useless exercise.

Anabaptist preachers and writers used a parable to emphasize the importance of like-mindedness. Here is one version as cited in the article, "The Lord's Supper," in *Mennonite Encyclopedia*:

> With the bread the unity among [all in the church] is symbolized. Where there are many small kernels of grain to be combined into one loaf there is need first to grind them and to make them into one flour . . . which can be achieved only through suffering. Just as Christ, our dear Lord, went before us, so too we want to follow him in like manner. And the bread symbolizes the unity of the [congregation].
>
> Likewise with the wine: many small grapes come together to make the one wine. That happens by means of the press, understood here as suffering. And thus also the wine indicates suffering. Hence, whoever wants to be in [congregational] union has to drink from the cup of the Lord, for this cup symbolizes suffering.

Suffering spoken was very real to the Anabaptists. Many were martyred for their conviction that the church is a voluntary fellowship of believers. They expressed this in and through the free celebration of the Lord's Supper outside the institutional church. For this they were persecuted.

We may not suffer the same kind of persecution. For some in other places in today's world, such persecution still occurs. Even for Christians in North America, the road to unity among

Christians and Christian groups is sometimes not an easy road. The road should not be avoided.

Thus we proclaim the Lord's death until he comes. The Lord's Supper is a celebration of hope. In celebrating the Lord's Supper we not only keep alive the remembrance of his death, but we also proclaim his coming again: "For as often as you eat this bread and drink the cup, you proclaim the Lord's death until he comes" (1 Corinthians 11:26).

We catch a note of excited anticipation of the future in Jesus' words to his disciples: "I have eagerly desired to eat the Passover with you before I suffer, for I tell you, I will not eat of it until it is fulfilled in the kingdom of God. Then he took a cup, and after giving thanks he said, 'Take this and divide it among yourselves, for I tell you that from now on I will not drink of the fruit of the vine until the kingdom of God comes'" (Luke 22:15–16). The Lord's Supper is a foretaste of the heavenly banquet yet to come.

Questions for Discussion

1. What distinguishes a Mennonite understanding of the Lord's Supper?
2. Explain how Jesus is present with us in the celebration of the Lord's Supper today.
3. Who should be invited to participate in the Lord's Supper?
4. Explore the themes of suffering, death and resurrection joy as these relate to the impact of the Lord's Supper on the life of the church community and the individual believer.

Foot Washing

The practice of washing feet has developed among some Mennonite groups. Foot washing as a ritual in Christian worship is done in response to the words of Jesus: "If I, your Lord and Teacher, have washed your feet, you also ought to wash one another's feet" (John 13:14). The ritual was fairly widespread in the Mennonite Church, but not as common in the General Conference. In our day some congregations are giving up this traditional practice while others are beginning to adopt it.

How is foot washing done? While there are variations, the ritual normally proceeds in the following way. Basins of water with a towel or two nearby are placed in several areas of the sanctuary or in separate rooms. One area is for the men, the other for the women. The ceremony is often done before or after the celebration of the Lord's Supper.

The invitation is given for persons to come to the designated areas. There individuals wash the feet of another person, and have their feet washed by another person. Sometimes this is done reciprocally, two by two. Often the congregation sings hymns during the ceremony. The "washing" tends to be a symbolic wetting of the feet, while the person places his or her feet over or in the basin. After the feet are dried, the two often embrace in an expression of Christian love.

Washing one another's feet has a sociological background in the Old Testament. In the sandy and dusty environment of the Middle East, it is typical to wear sandals or go barefoot. Inevitably one's feet need to be washed often and certainly upon entering a house. Offering facilities for foot washing and even stooping to wash the feet of a visitor is a sign of welcome and hospitality.

Remember the story of Abraham and Sarah who were visited by three messengers who brought the old couple news from the Lord that a son would be born to them. Abraham welcomed them with the words, "Let a little water be brought, and wash your feet, and rest yourselves under the tree"(Genesis 18:4). With this gesture he was saying, "You are welcome here. I'm at your service." This was a typical act of courtesy in Old Testament times.

We believe that Jesus Christ calls us to serve one another in love as he did. As sometimes happens with everyday practices, the habit of foot washing took on meaning far beyond the need to enter a house with clean feet. Already in the example of Abraham, it was a gesture of welcome. More can be said. The host needed to kneel before the guests to accomplish the task. So washing the strangers' feet was a sign of humility and servanthood.

Jesus came as a servant. He served us by taking our sins upon himself and thus giving us a new lease on life. Thus it is not surprising that he employed the ritual of foot washing to emphasize his role. He insisted on washing the feet of Peter. When Peter objected to having Jesus wash his feet, Jesus said, "You do not know now what I am doing, but later you will understand" (John 13:7). And he added, "Unless I wash you, you have no share with me" (v. 8).

How do the disciples have a share in him if and when he washes their feet? First, they (we) need to receive the benefit of the atonement for sin that Jesus accomplished on earth. Second, the disciples—then and now—need to follow his lead and become servants as well. In this way they (we) share in his servile life. In other words, Jesus needed to serve by bearing the cross in Peter's behalf before Peter would be freed to share in a life of Christ-empowered service. Footwashing symbolizes these spiritual teachings.

When Jesus had finished the foot washing ritual, he said,

"Do you know what I have done to you? . . . If I, your Lord and Teacher, have washed your feet, you also ought to wash one another's feet. For I have set you an example, that you also should do as I have done to you" (John 13:12,14–15). In a lesser way than Christ, yet in a similar way, we are "Christ" to others when we serve them in his name. The motto of Mennonite Central Committee comes to mind: "Service in the name of Christ."

Jesus stooped to wash the disciples' feet. Stooping is not a position we moderns assume easily. It is not popular to humble ourselves. In our culture we place high value on self-assertion, on power, on individual worth. Our society and our educational system tend to create me-centred individuals who have little patience with self-negation. Foot washing does not fit readily into modern culture. To speak of humbling ourselves sounds like a set-up for getting stepped on.

The gesture of stooping helps us grasp the significance of Jesus humbling himself to come to earth. "Though he was in the form of God, he did not regard equality with God as something to be exploited, but emptied himself, taking the form of a slave, being born in human likeness" (Philippians 2:6–7). John 1:14 says: "The Word became flesh and lived among us." The move from heaven to earth required a self-emptying. The hymn, "See Amid the Winter's Snow," has the lines, "Low within a manger lies / He who built the starry skies."

Throughout the New Testament, Jesus' self-emptying is a message not only about the incarnation of the Christ-child. It is also about people in high and in low places, proud people and humble people. Before his birth, Mary the mother of Jesus said of him, "His mercy is for those who fear him from generation to generation. . . . He has scattered the proud in the thoughts of their hearts. He has brought down the powerful from their thrones, and lifted up the lowly (Luke 1:50–52). The call to humble service is a strong theme in the Scriptures. It cuts in all directions, including economics: "So therefore none of you can become my disciples if you do not give up all your possessions" (Luke 14:33).

Some Bible scholars suggest that in the New Testament foot washing is linked with the preparation of bodies for burial. There was the event at the home of Lazarus and Mary and Martha. During the meal Mary took some costly perfume with which she anointed Jesus' feet, and then wiped them with her hair. Jesus hints that Mary is doing this in preparation for his burial (John 12:7).

In the next chapter, which has the report of Jesus washing the disciples' feet, Jesus continues to speak of the cross as though the foot washing ritual is somehow linked to his death. In the one other place where foot washing is mentioned in the New Testament, it refers to the assignment of widows in the church to "wash the feet of the saints" (1 Timothy 5:10). This could refer to preparing the dead for burial.

Jesus' teachings build a close connection between death and servanthood. He says to his disciples, "Whoever wishes to be great among you must be your servant, and whoever wishes to be first among you must be your slave; just as the Son of Man came not to be served but to serve, and to give his life a ransom for many" (Matthew 20:26–28). The "dying" of which he speaks includes not only physical death, but also a life of dying to self and service to others.

Believers who wash each other's feet show that they share in the body of Christ. When Jesus said to Peter, "Unless I wash you, you have no share with me" (John 13:8), he was preparing Peter for life in the church. In chapter 9 we defined the church as the body of Christ. In line with that definition we can interpret Jesus' words to point to the believers' participation in the fellowship of the people of God. Thus Jesus' words highlight the importance of serving one another in the church.

The following texts highlight the call to the spiritual discipline of identifying with Christ in humility and service:

Do nothing from selfish ambition or conceit, but in humility regard others as better than yourselves. Let each of you look not to your own interests but to the interests of others. Let the same mind be in you that was in Jesus Christ, who . . . emptied himself, taking the form of a slave . . . and became obedient to the point of death—even death on a cross (Philippians 2:3–8).

We who are strong ought to put up with the failings of the weak, and not to please ourselves. Each of us must please the neighbor for the good purpose of building up the neighbor. For Christ did not please himself; but, as it is written, "The insults of those who insult you have fallen on me.". . . May the God of steadfastness and encouragement grant you to live in harmony with one another, in accordance with Jesus Christ, so that together you may with one voice glorify the God and Father of our Lord Jesus Christ (Romans 15:1–6).

At that time the disciples came to Jesus and asked, "Who is the greatest in the kingdom of heaven?" He called a child, whom he put among them, and said, "Truly I tell you, unless you change and become like children, you will never enter the kingdom of heaven. Whoever becomes humble like this child is the greatest in the kingdom of heaven. Whoever welcomes one such child in my name welcomes me" (Matthew 18:1–5).

Questions for Discussion

1. Study the biblical texts which speak to the practice of foot washing (*Confession,* page 53). What do you learn from these texts?
2. What spiritual meanings are conveyed with the practice of foot washing?
3. What do we give and what do we receive in washing another's feet? Which is the more difficult?
4. Reflect on humility and sober self-evaluation using texts like Philippians 2:3–8; Romans 15:1–6; Matthew 18:1–5; Psalm 8; Romans 12: 3–5.

14

Discipline in the Church

Every religion and every society has behavioural requirements. It "comes with the furniture." You can't form a community without some do's and don'ts that everyone needs to respect and follow. Christian faith also comes with a set of expectations for its adherents. These may vary from group to group, depending on how the Scriptures are interpreted. Some congregations emphasize common expectations for all members. Others allow a great deal of individual freedom. Church discipline is a familiar topic for Christians.

The topic of discipline is unsettling for some people. People of an older generation remember a time when the church dealt more strictly with its members than the congregation does today. Some wish for a return of that earlier style when right and wrong were clearly defined. Others do not. They tell negative stories of being excluded from church membership on certain moral and ethical grounds that appear less clear today.

People of the younger generation, and also some in the older category, sometimes don't like the idea of deciding how other people should behave. The younger generation has grown up in the midst of a society whose philosophy is "live and let live." Let other people do what they want to as long as what they do does not harm or disturb me. Disciplining others in the church sounds especially hard, since it appears we are then deciding on their spiritual fate. This becomes a rather serious matter.

It is important to begin our affirmation of discipline at the right place. Discipline is rooted in God's election of a people that is to be holy before God and in the midst of the world. This calls for church communities where people hold each other accountable for how they conduct their personal lives.

Some translations of the Bible use the expression "a peculiar people" to emphasize the uniqueness of the people of God. The expectation is that God's elected people will be different from what is popular in society. In turn this will have an effect upon people around us. You can't exert an influence in society if you merely imitate everyone else. No one would even notice.

We believe that the practice of discipline in the church is a sign of God's offer of forgiveness and transforming grace to believers who are moving away from faithful discipleship or who have been overtaken by sin. Church discipline has its background in God's election and God's salvation. We find an Old Testament summary of this background in Exodus 19:3–6:

> Then Moses went up to God; and the Lord called to him out of the mountain, saying, "Thus you shall say to the house of Jacob, and tell the people of Israel: You have seen what I did to the Egyptians, and how I bore you on eagles' wings and brought you to myself. Now therefore, if you obey my voice and keep my covenant, you shall be my treasured possession out of all the peoples. Indeed, the earth is mine, but you shall be for me a priestly kingdom and a holy nation. These are the words that you shall speak to the children of Israel.

The New Testament continues this emphasis in passages such as the following:

> But you are a chosen race, a royal priesthood, a holy nation, God's own people, in order that you may proclaim the mighty acts of him who called you out of darkness into his marvelous light. Once you were not a people, but now you are God's people; once you had not received mercy, but now you have received mercy (1 Peter 2:9–10).

In its disciplined life, the church shall be an instrument of the grace of God. The object of discipline is to urge people not to follow destructive ways of life, but to enjoy God's salvation. It follows that if discipline is to achieve its goal, it must be done in a spirit of grace and forgiveness.

People sometimes have the impression that in exercising discipline the church is on a power trip, as though the whole purpose is to come down hard on people and be judgmental. But the focus of these texts is on grace and mercy. The intent is to offer grace and forgiveness to people who are headed in the wrong direction. The hope is that persons will repent (literally, turn around) and head in the right direction. The purpose is not to impose "a punishment to fit the crime." Rather, the goal is to heal brokenness and give reconciliation a chance.

According to the teaching of Jesus Christ and the apostles, all believers participate in the church's mutual care and discipline as appropriate. Jesus taught a simple and neat pattern of church discipline. We find this in Matthew 18. The instruction concerning discipline (vv. 15–20) is preceded by reminders about becoming humble like children (vv. 1–5), not being judgmental (vv. 6–9) and seeking the lost sheep (vv. 10–14). The instruction is followed by a question from Peter about how many times one should forgive (vv. 21–22) and the parable of the unforgiving servant (vv. 23–35). What could be clearer as to the purpose of admonition?

The first step in the process of discipline is for the person who is wronged to speak to the one who is said to have done something wrong (v. 15). If things are clarified, confessed and forgiven, the matter is settled. "If you forgive the sins of any, they are forgiven them; if you retain the sins of any, they are retained" (John 20:23). The member remains in good standing in the church. The matter need be taken no further. Even though the situation is taken care of privately, it was done on behalf of the entire church.

A second step is required if the person spoken to will not listen: one brings along one or two witnesses (Matthew 18:16). This step is invoked only if the person-to-person approach does not yield results. The point of the witnesses is to verify what is said and to ensure that, if the conversation gets intense, someone is present to regulate the situation and to safeguard the truth. This step is in line with Old Testament procedure: "A single witness shall not be sufficient to convict a person of any crime or wrongdoing in connection with any offense that may be committed. Only on the evidence of two or three witnesses shall a charge be sustained" (Deuteronomy 19:15).

In this second step the spirit in which one approaches the encounter is still crucial. The apostle Paul speaks of seeking restoration in ". . . a spirit of gentleness" (Galatians 6:1). The added warning to ". . . take care that you yourselves are not tempted" (6:1) probably refers to the temptation to become angry and judgmental, perhaps even violent.

Step three comes into play if the person still will not listen. This step entails taking the matter to the church. Jesus does not say whether the erring person appears before the church or only before those who speak concerning the situation. That could be flexible, depending upon the situation. This step is taken in the hope that the person will listen to the church's words of admonition. If the person heeds the advice of the church, good. If not, "let such a one be to you as a Gentile and a tax collector" (Matthew 18:17). In other words, the fellowship is broken, at least for the time being.

Jesus leaves us with a helpful pattern to be used in approaching one another when things go wrong between and among people in the church. The pattern as such does not fit every situation. Yet it leaves us with biblical principles for church practice today.

Mutual encouragement, pastoral care and discipline should normally lead to confession, forgiveness and reconciliation. "Discipline" and "discipleship" belong to the same family of words. The root meaning is "to lead" or "to teach." At its best, the aim of discipline is to provide a pathway of learning that helps persons mature in their discipleship. Successful learning usually involves difficulties of some kind. This may include such things as letting go of old habits or sacrificing pleasure for the discipline of skill training.

Positive encouragement is an important element in discipline. Learning occurs best in a supportive environment. Discipline is accepted more readily when surrounded by grace rather than by judgment. The ten commandments, religious "disciplines" of the people of Israel, come with the promise that God is much longer on showing steadfast love than on punishment (Exodus 20:5–6). In the same spirit, the Ephesian church encouraged as follows: "Speaking the truth in love, we are to grow up in every way into him who is the head, into Christ" (Ephesians 4:15).

If the erring member persists in sin without repentance and rejects even the admonition of the congregation, membership should be suspended. There is a serious note to discipline. Truth and untruth cannot live together. Do we wait for the Day of the Lord before addressing issues of wrongdoing? As we have seen, Jesus calls us to be pro-active in dealing with sin. Hopefully the admonition is accepted. If it is not, the congregation should act, depending on the gravity of the sin. But action should not be taken lightly. Relationships are at stake. It is sobering to realize that the congregation is instructed to act on God's behalf: "Truly I tell you, whatever you bind on earth will be bound in heaven, and whatever you loose on earth will be loosed in heaven" (Matthew 18:18).

This is why discipline must not be taken lightly. The pain felt by the person being corrected is everyone's pain. There should be a readiness to forgive and to console the person and to affirm love for the person (2 Corinthians 2:7–8). At all times, we are to lean toward mercy rather than judgment, to restoration rather than to exclusion. We are to forgive because Christ has been merciful toward us.

We acknowledge that discipline, rightly understood and practised, undergirds the integrity of the church's witness in word and deed. The New Testament sets a high ideal for the church. "Christ loved the church . . . so as to present the church to himself in splendor, without a spot or wrinkle or anything of the kind—yes, so that she might be holy and without blemish" (Ephesians 5:25,27). Notice that Christ's concern for the pure church is motivated by love for the church. We must take care that zeal for purity does not overshadow love for erring brothers and sisters. It takes an overflowing measure of God's grace to rightly understand and practice discipline.

Questions for Discussion

1. What are positive reasons for mutual admonition in the church?
2. How do discipline and grace work together?
3. Outline the steps in discipline according to Matthew 18:15–20. How would this apply in the church in our day? How are caring and discipline related?
4. Is forgiveness possible in every situation, or does it have limitations? In your experience, how long does forgiveness take?
5. Give personal examples of the miracle of reconciliation.

Ministry and Leadership

Is Christian ministry the responsibility of only some, or of all? How will I know if I am called to take a leadership role in the church? What do we believe about ministry and leadership?

We believe that ministry continues the work of Christ who, through the Holy Spirit, gives gifts to all believers and empowers them for service in the church and in the world. What is ministry? The answer is simple yet all-encompassing. Ministry is the continuation of the work of Christ. When we take up the work Jesus instructed us to do, we are engaged in ministry. What is this work? It certainly includes the following: to give food to the hungry and drink to the thirsty; to welcome strangers; to care for the sick; and to minister to those in prison (Matthew 25:31–46). It also includes the work of building up the body of Christ through activities such as teaching, preaching, evangelizing and pastoring (Ephesians 4:12).

Every Christian is called to ministry. The calling need not be official with ordination and a church job. "Each of us was given grace according to the measure of Christ's gift" (Ephesians 4:7). In some cases Christian ministry is nothing more than a gesture of friendship offered almost without thinking about it. In other cases Christian ministry is a lifetime vocation consciously chosen. Both are contributions to ministry. Every Christian qualifies for Christian ministry. "Like good stewards of the manifold grace of God, serve one another with whatever gift each of you has received" (1 Peter 4:10).

We are endowed and empowered for ministry through the Holy Spirit. This connection of ministry to the Holy Spirit is profound. Leaders and people who minister need grace for their responsibilities. They also need strength to face the temptations that come with the role of leadership. Some people are too modest to think of themselves as fit for Christian ministry. But their calling is not negated by their modesty. Their suitability for ministry does not depend on their perceived ability. The Holy Spirit is given to each and to all. God can take the least likely instrument and shape it into a channel of blessing.

There is also the other extreme. Some people allow their pride to spoil their contribution to Christian ministry. Perhaps they could serve well but the self gets in the way. The gifts we bring to ministry are God-given gifts. We may not boast as though our ministry were our accomplishment for our credit. The Holy Spirit reminds people they need to serve with a submissive spirit.

Ministry comes in two parts. It is carried out in the church and in the world. Both are important. Ministry in the church focuses on speaking to people who have joined the church. Ministry in the world is offered to people who are not part of the church community. In the world, ministry takes the form of evangelism and Christian service. Some persons are called to equip the believers; others are gifted in reaching out to the needy. A congregation should strike a fair balance between ministry inward and ministry outward. Neither should be neglected. Both should be valued.

We also believe that God calls particular persons in the church to specific leadership ministries and offices. In the Roman Catholic church spiritual leaders are chosen and given their assignments by central authorities. In Mennonite churches the pastors are chosen by local congregations, a practice begun by the Anabaptists when they broke with the Roman church. For Anabaptists this was a return to the original way of the New Testament church. In choosing leaders from among the group, it was of crucial importance that congregational members should be agreed among themselves who would be their leaders.

The call to ministerial leadership is a high and important calling. The task is to equip the church members for the work of ministry (Ephesians 4:12). According to the apostle Paul, bishops (or overseers) of the church have a "noble" assignment (1 Timothy 3:1). The ethical demands upon such a person are high: "A bishop must be above reproach, married only once, temperate, sensible, respectable, hospitable, an apt teacher, not a drunkard, not violent but gentle, not quarrelsome, and not a lover of money" (3:2–3). And there is more. No question about it. Leaders are expected to take the lead in moral and ethical matters.

Young people are often included among candidates for ministry. It is thought that Jesus' disciples were mostly young adults. They became the first apostles, key leaders in the early church. Jeremiah was only a youth when he was chosen to be a prophet of Israel (Jeremiah 1:4–10). The apostle Paul encourages the young Timothy: "Let no one despise your youth, but set the believers an example in speech and conduct, in love, in faith, in purity" (1 Timothy 4:12). The early leaders of the Anabaptist movement were mostly in their 20s.

Today's youth should give serious consideration to the call to particular ministries in and through the church. These may include the range from full-time paid positions to part-time voluntary assignments. The church needs the perspective of the younger generation. God can speak in new ways through those who come with fresh enthusiasm and new ideas. At the same time members of the congregation do well to encourage young people who are able and willing to provide leadership. The congregation should be sure to give young people some space to practice their gifts and to experiment with their creative ideas.

Church leaders sometimes struggle with question of their role. Do they follow the wishes of the congregation and the wider church at all costs? Do they give singular attention to the will of God alone? Should they follow their own best wisdom and their conscience? What if church and God and self seem to give conflicting signals?

For example, there may be a conflict among members in the congregation. The leader knows the truth about the conflict. A word from God is needed in the situation. Yet influential people in the congregation suggest that nothing should be said, since a word of judgment on the part of the pastor would alienate people further and cause an irreparable rift. What should be the role of the pastor in this situation?

In some New Testament texts women are named among the persons in leadership roles in the church. They prophesy (Acts 2:17–18); they minister for the Lord (Romans 16:3–16). In other texts women are advised to remain silent in the church (1 Corinthians 14:34–36). We should note two things. First, Jesus never commands women to remain silent. Rather he converses with them and shows respect for them. Second, when the apostle Paul gives the silencing word to women, it is said for the sake of peace. In a culture where men rule, the emancipation of women does not occur without a backlash. At such times it is better to work in a peacemaking manner over time than to provoke violence. For this reason the apostle calls on women to be patient. We must hasten to add that such a situation gives men no right to act in a domineering way.

All who minister are accountable to God and to the community of faith as they serve the church.   The word "ministry" brings to mind ministers or pastors of congregations. We assume that the responsibility for ministry rests with our church leaders. Although the function of church leaders is vital to the church, the primary responsibility for ministry rests with the church itself, not with certain individuals in its midst. Ministry belongs to the whole church. The church in ministry is like a body with many functions. Each person is a function of the body, like a thumb or an ear or a hand. Ministry is the task of the entire church and of all persons in the church.

Fellow laborers with me in the ministry,
  Guardians and trumpeters are they,
  Spiritual pillars are they,
  Messengers of peace are they called
  Bishops and overseers are they called,
  Shepherds are they called,
  Teachers are they called,
  The light of the world are they called,
  The salt of the earth are they called,
  Ministers are they called in Christ's stead.
  Brothers and sisters serve
    but do not lord it.
              —Adapted from Menno Simons

Church leaders are grasped by two passions: to serve the Lord and to serve the church. Ministers preach the word of God in the midst of the congregation. They are faithful readers and interpreters of the Scriptures for these times. In fulfilling this role, they are representatives of God. At the same time, ministers have a heart-to-heart relationship with the church as a whole and with each member of the congregation. Preaching and counselling grow out of this closeness with God and passionate care for the people of God.

The congregation must give prayerful attention to the calling and ordination of its ministers. The apostle Paul tells Timothy, "Do not ordain anyone hastily" (1 Timothy 5:22). To ordain means to give a person the awesome task of serving in a specific role on behalf of the church. Such an assignment should not be taken lightly. Give everyone time to express their views on the appropriateness of the person for the task. Allow the Holy Spirit to guide the process. Sometimes churches become anxious and act hastily when they do not have an appointed leader. But it is better to have a sense of peace about the decision than to rush into it. The ordination should not be taken lightly. It is noteworthy that the ordination of Aaron and his sons was an event that lasted for seven days (Exodus 29:35).

An important role of persons in pastoral ministry is preaching. The sermon is a versatile instrument for the proclamation of the faith. It has at least three functions: teaching, evangelizing and prophesying. A teaching sermon deepens the people's understanding of Scripture. Evangelistic preaching confronts persons with the need to make an initial decision for Christ or to renew a commitment to Christ. Prophetic preaching entails the interpretation of current events in light of Scripture. This helps believers orient their lives faithfully to the future. Preaching is a great privilege and an awesome responsibility!

Teamwork is the key word in ministry. In a typical congregation there are many leaders. Each has a role to play. One plants the seed. Another waters the plant. Another harvests the fruit. The church is like a garden that requires tending at every stage. We should be sensitive to the many contributions that are required for spiritual life to flourish. Only a part of the work is done "on stage" by persons who lead church services and church meetings. Countless contributions are made in quiteness "behind the scenes." When all is said and done, "only God gives the growth" (1 Corinthians 3:7).

Questions for Discussion

1. How does the church understand ministry, and whose task is it?
2. How are ministerial leaders chosen in your congregation? Does the practice work well? Would you consider the calling to become a minister?
3. Who should be invited to ministerial leadership? What are the necessary qualifications? Which men and women in your congregation meet these?
4. What are the implications of the statement that "ministry belongs to the whole church" (page 87)?
5. What are your expectations of pastors and other ministerial leaders in your congregation? What are your responsibilities toward ministerial leaders?

Church Order and Unity

According to 1996 statistics, the Christian population of the world amounts to 1,955,229,000. This is 33.7 percent of the world's population of 5,804,121,000 people. This Christian population is spread throughout all countries of the world. Even though you and I will see only a fraction of this multitude of Christians in our lifetime, together we are one spiritual body. We are one in our common acceptance of Jesus Christ as revealed in the Scriptures and in our ecumenical confession as expressed in the Apostles' Creed.

Besides this living community of people, we can add countless Christians who have already died and have proceeded to their eternal place of rest. We should also add those of Old Testament times who died in hope of the fulfilment of God's promise. They too belong to the spiritual community of the church of Jesus Christ. We are united in one body with all who have preceded us in faith and hope in former generations. What a parade!

The Christian church is comprised of three major families: the Orthodox, the Catholics and Protestants. Most believers fit easily into one of these three groups. Yet some do not wish to be placed into one or the other of these groupings. For example, Mennonites have been depicted at times as "neither Catholic nor Protestant."

Within the Protestant family, members are organized into congregations (local groups), conferences (groupings of congregations) and denominations (large structured church organizations). Can these structures give witness to the truth that "God is a God not of disorder but of peace" (1 Corinthians 14:33)?

We believe that the church of Jesus Christ is one body, with many members, ordered in such a way that, through the one Spirit, believers may be built spiritually into a dwelling place for God. Should Christians be concerned about the unity of the church? Yes. The author of Ephesians says, "Make every effort to maintain the unity of the Spirit in the bond of peace" (Ephesians 4:3). It is the biblical responsibility of each local congregation and each larger group to do what is practically possible to relate in a Christian spirit to those who claim the same Spirit. Opportunities to practice gracious inter-church relationships in our neighbourhoods and in our countries are limitless. "How very good and pleasant it is when kindred live together in unity!" (Psalm 133:1).

Where there was disunity in the early church, it was mainly because of the issue of race relations. Could Jews and Gentiles worship the same Lord? Could the various Gentile nationalities take the Lord's Supper together? The apostle Peter learned a lesson about race relations when he was led by the Holy Spirit to the house of Cornelius (Acts 10). There he taught Cornelius and his household about Jesus. Peter also received an insight through that encounter. At the end of the experience he said: "I truly understand that God shows no partiality, but in every nation anyone who fears him and does what is right is acceptable to him. You know the message he sent to the people of Israel, preaching peace by Jesus Christ—he is Lord of all" (Acts 10:34–36). The lesson to Peter and to us is that people from every nation are acceptable to God. We should look down on no one. Our mission is to spread the good news of God's peace to all.

Each congregation and denomination takes a unique role and occupies an important space on the face of the earth. This is in accordance with the words in Ephesians:

> Each of us was given grace according to the measure of Christ's gift . . . to equip the saints for the work of ministry, for building up the body of Christ, until all of us come to the unity

of the faith and of the knowledge of the Son of God, to maturity, to the measure of the full stature of Christ (Ephesians 4:7,12–13).

This text can be applied positively to our separate denominations. Each is given grace and gifts by Christ. Each has a ministry in the progress toward maturity in Christ. Each church group has a role to play in Christian witness in the world.

There is an intimate connection between unity among Christians and their witness in the world. Jesus points to this connection when he prays to the Father:

As you, Father, are in me and I am in you, may they also be in us, so that the world may believe that you have sent me. The glory that you have given me I have given them, so that they may be one, as we are one, I in them and you in me, that they may become completely one, so that the world may know that you have sent me and have loved them even as you have loved me (John 17:21–23).

As God's people, the church is a holy temple, a spiritual house, founded upon the apostles and prophets, with Christ Jesus himself as the cornerstone. The Bible compares God's people to a house. This helps to emphasize the unity of the church. The temple of the Old Testament was called "the house of the Lord" (Psalm 42:4). It was the place where the ark of the covenant was kept, in which the Ten Commandments were stored. The Commandments and other Old Testament Scriptures provided a blueprint for the faith and life of the people.

When the people gathered in and about the temple they truly felt they were a spiritual family and the temple was their spiritual home. The temple was special because it was the house of the Lord, the dwelling place of God. The temple was a reflection of the created world in which and over which God ruled the universe.

The image of the temple is carried forward into the New Testament. The people of Christ are described as God's temple in whom God's Spirit dwells (1 Corinthians 3:16–17). The church is constructed of "living stones . . . built into a spiritual house" (1 Peter 2:5). The cornerstone of the spiritual building is Jesus Christ. In an actual building the cornerstone is shaped and laid in such a way that it indicates the direction of the length and the breadth and the verticle line of the entire structure. In the same way, Jesus Christ sets the spiritual direction for his people.

House builders know the importance of unity and order. A secure building must be carefully planned and methodically constructed. One begins by digging downward to find a secure foundation. Only then can the walls be erected. In the same way, after it has been firmly established that "no other foundation can anyone lay than that which is laid, which is Jesus Christ" (1 Corinthians 3:11), we can begin to build on this foundation.

Spiritually, the foundation of the church is the report and interpretation of Jesus found in the work of the apostles and prophets (Ephesians 2:20). The apostles were disciples who had been with Jesus personally. They saw what he did and heard what he taught. We can depend on them for a true report concerning Jesus Christ. Paul was added because on the road to Damascus he had received a special vision of Jesus.

The prophets were the Old Testament preachers who provided the pre-interpretation of God's revelation in Christ. In the New Testament church the role of prophecy continued in the role of preachers who interpreted the teachings and actions of Jesus for the present and for the future (Acts 10:32). The apostles and prophets provided unity and order for Christian beliefs and practices.

In making decisions, whether to choose leaders or resolve issues, members of the church listen and speak in a spirit of prayerful openness, with the Scriptures as the constant guide. One of the earliest struggles in the early church resulted in a one-issue conference at Jerusalem. The question was whether to require the Gentiles to obey all the traditional rules contained in the Jewish instructions of the Old Testament. The result of the conference was positive in that the church representatives came to a peaceable agreement which was based on the Scriptures as they understood them.

The proceedings, which are described in Acts 15:1–21, have been used as an example of how the church should deliberate. The conference included debate, testimony of Gentile conversions, an appeal by a respected leader (Peter), a time of silence, intense listening, the reading of Scripture, and a time of testing a proposal brought forward by one of the leaders (James). This is a remarkable story of a decision-making process. In the end, several delegates were sent to share their findings with the Gentiles who rejoiced when they heard the results.

The church is a variety of assemblies which meet regularly, including local congregations and larger conferences. Imagine a missionary congregation begun by the apostle Paul and his coworkers. The local believers sign in as members. Soon they realize their need for belonging to a network of congregations. Paul, who has remained among them to establish the group, tells them of the other congregations that have been formed throughout Asia Minor. The newly formed congregation rejoices in this sense of the wider fellowship.

The group decides to choose leaders from its midst. Believers from neighbouring congregations are invited to share in the blessing on the occasion of the commissioning service. Together with these other congregations, the group affirms one Lord, one faith, one baptism. Paul leaves, and the group awaits a letter from him. When a letter arrives, it is read to the congregation, along with the greetings. The letter is then carried to the neighbouring congregation, where it is also read in public before it is passed on to yet another church. In these ways the body of Christ expands and also unites.

Today we find numerous church groupings of Mennonite congregations. In some countries, such as Taiwan, there is only one Mennonite conference. In others, such as Canada, there are numerous conferences. On some continents, such as Europe, North America and South America, conferences sometimes cut across national boundaries. In other countries, they are contained within the country.

Larger church groupings, such as conferences, serve an important function. They provide an extended church family for members and congregations. Such a family is important for promoting a common Anabaptist-Mennonite connection; for upholding the commitment to a holistic interpretation of the Scriptures; for supporting church leaders who know and encourage one another; and the list goes on. Conferences provide a "foundation" of support for those ministries which all congregations desire to do together. This includes an educational program, home mission, youth work, and more.

A conference also opens a window of opportunity for its members to spread the light of Christ beyond the local congregation. The church unites its voice in speaking to issues in society and in reaching out through international mission.

Questions for Discussion

1. What is the special contribution that the Mennonite church should make in the midst of the world's many Christian denominations? What can it learn from other denominations?
2. What are the forces that caused disunity in the church of the New Testament? What causes disunity in the congregation today?
3. Where does (or should) the church find its basis for unity?
4. Study the decision-making process in Acts 15:1–12. What can we learn from this account?
5. Share experiences of spiritual inspiration gained in larger church gatherings such as conferences, conventions and retreats.

The Apostles' Creed

I believe in God, the Father almighty,
  creator of heaven and earth;
I believe in Jesus Christ,
    God's only Son, our Lord,
    who was conceived by the Holy Spirit,
    born of the Virgin Mary,
    suffered under Pontius Pilate,
    was crucified, died, and was buried;
he descended to the dead.
On the third day he arose again;
he ascended into heaven,
he is seated at the right hand of the Father,
    and he will come again to judge
    the living and the dead.
I believe in the Holy Spirit,
  the holy catholic church,
  the communion of saints,
  the forgiveness of sins,
  the resurrection of the body,
  and the life everlasting.

Discipleship and the Christian Life

Christians everywhere accept the Scriptures and the early creeds as the basic foundation of faith. Beyond that, however, every denomination seems to have its special emphasis. For the Lutherans it's grace. For the Pentecostals it's the Holy Spirit. For the Catholics it's confession. For the Mennonites it's discipleship. We take seriously Jesus' words, "Follow me." The Sermon on the Mount is our favourite text. "Service in the name of Christ" is our slogan.

We believe that Jesus Christ calls us to take up our cross and follow him. The motivation for discipleship is Jesus Christ. We follow him not because it will bring us reward. Not because it makes us feel good. Not because we fear punishment. Rather, following Jesus is the normal way of expressing our devotion to him. We follow Christ because he is Lord. We follow because he said, "Follow me." How else would we indicate that Christ is ours and we belong to him?

The Greek word for discipling means learning. To follow Jesus as a disciple is to enrol as a student in the school of Christ. The disciples who followed him understood their little community to be a travelling classroom. They learned from Jesus as they watched him deal with live situations. They gathered around him afterwards for interpretive lectures and for question-and-answer periods. The program of studies unfolded as they followed him in the way.

The school of learning offered by Jesus was no easy course. Jesus emphasized the hardness of the way. A would-be follower said to Jesus: "I will follow you wherever you go" (Luke 9:57). Jesus replied with the reminder that "the Son of Man has nowhere to lay his head" (9:58). The emphasis is on total devotion to one purpose only. "No one who puts a hand to the plough and looks back is fit for the kingdom of God" (9:62). Learning and commmitment go hand in hand.

What is involved in following Jesus today? Where are the pathways of life that offer discipleship training? What does it take to remain faithful in difficult situations? Who will say, "I want to know Christ and the power of his resurrection and the sharing of his sufferings by becoming like him in his death" (Philippians 3:10)?

The experience of God through the Holy Spirit, prayer, Scripture and the church empowers us and teaches us how to follow Christ. We follow Christ not in our own strength but with the help of spiritual sources which surround us and are available to us. Through the Holy Spirit, Christ is constantly present with us. We know this presence when we find courage to speak the truth or when we overcome fear. Through prayer we are in touch with God at every moment. To the Christian prayer is like breathing. The Scriptures provide an inexhaustible source of guidance when we come to forks in the road. Members of the church provide a community of support for those who would be faithful. The church's programs offer numerous opportunities to serve and learn.

Our discipleship is lived out "in Christ." Positioning ourselves in Christ requires a two-sided sensitivity. The centre area is the place of the Christian's pilgrimage. We carry our cross within the protection of Christ who bore his cross on our behalf and gives us a cross to carry. Christ does not leave us alone but helps us to bear our cross.

Our life in Christ is upheld by two energizers. The first is the gift of God's grace which removes our sin and guilt and constantly renews our spirits with the message that we are indeed children of God. It would be a mistake to claim grace as an excuse for continuing in sin or as an affirmation that we are nothing while God is everything. Rather, grace frees us from such bondage and energizes us. Grace, rightly understood and grasped, sustains our life in Christ.

The second energizer is the context of responsibilities into which God places us in life. Humans are wonderfully created with the wisdom and the initiative to serve God by serving others in life. All was not lost with the Fall. God's offer of forgiveness and invitation to new beginnings provides sufficient encouragement for new life in Christ. It would be a mistake to claim human possibilities apart from God, the Giver of life. Human potentiality is sustained in the context of the worship of God.

To sustain our life in Christ requires a delicate balance between dependence on God's forgiveness and on God's empowerment. Reliance on forgiveness frees us from an overly negative attitude about ourselves. Reliance on God's empowerment frees us from an overly positive assessment of our own worth. There is the temptation, on the one hand, to think too lowly of ourselves, relying only on the grace of forgiveness for our rescue. There is the temptation, on the other hand, to think too highly of ourselves and thus attempt again, as Adam and Eve did, to worship the creature rather than the Creator. To keep our balance is the key. "I can do all things through Christ who strengthens me" (Philippians 4:13).

Our participation in Christ includes both salvation and discipleship.   To be free to live as we were meant to live requires that we become free in two directions. First, we need to be freed from the grim grip of sin and evil. Second, we need to be freed for joyous life and creativity. In the salvation which Christ brings, both freedoms are offered us. He rescues us from the grip of sin by conquering the evil powers that threaten life and by taking our sin upon himself. He rescues us from the chaos of confused existence by opening up a pathway of activity that promises creative life and deeply satisfying joy.

We usually link the first of these freedoms with salvation

and the second with discipleship. Actually, we are free to speak of the second part, which entails following Jesus, as part of the experience of salvation also. This what the apostle Paul refers to with the words: "Work out your own salvation with fear and trembling; for it is God who is at work in you, enabling you both to will and to work for his good pleasure" (Philippians 2:12b–13). In discipleship we are saved from meaningless existence. Our feet are put upon a pathway of life that leads to righteousness.

Conformity to Christ necessarily implies nonconformity to the world. From a human standpoint it is normal to serve ourselves and to give our devotion to things that will provide a quick fix. Joshua stood before the people of Israel and announced, "As for me and my household, we will serve the Lord" (Joshua 24:15).

From a human standpoint, it is the rich and powerful who rule kingdoms. Yet Jesus said, "Blessed are the poor in spirit, for theirs is the kingdom of heaven" (Matthew 5:3). I think of Albert Schweitzer who devoted his life energy to serving the poor in Africa.

From a human standpoint, it is natural to concern ourselves with the physical necessities of life. Yet Jesus taught his disciples, "Do not worry about your life, what you will eat or what you will drink, or about your body, what you will wear. Is not life more than food, and the body more than clothing?" (Matthew 6:25). I think of Mother Theresa who cast aside any concern for her own welfare and served the physical and spiritual needs of the dying on the streets of Calcutta.

From a human standpoint it was not natural for Jesus to go the way of suffering and death. Yet he prayed, "Not what I will but what you want" (Matthew 26:39). I think of Felix Mantz, an early Anabaptist, who risked his life for the truth of Scripture and was swallowed up by the Limmat River.

From a human standpoint, our inclination is to preserve life at all costs. Yet the apostle Paul wrote to the church at Rome,

"I appeal to you therefore, brothers and sisters, by the mercies of God, to present your bodies as a living sacrifice, holy and acceptable to God, which is your spiritual worship" (Romans 12:1).

It is no simple task to do the right thing, to live life in the Christian lane. Yet this is the challenge that faces the faithful church. Jesus said, "Enter through the narrow gate; for the gate is wide and the road is easy that leads to destruction, and there are many who take it. For the gate is narrow and the road is hard that leads to life, and there are few who find it" (Matthew 7:13–14).

In all areas of life we are called to be Jesus' disciples. God is all in all. Every nook and cranny of the created world is ours to claim and to enjoy. But the enjoyment will be temporary if we live as though life belongs to us. Deep satisfaction comes to us if and when we live in creation as God intended us to, "to the praise of his glory."

The Old Testament people were told by their prophets what it takes to live as God intended them to. "He has told you, O mortal, what is good; and what does the Lord require of you but to do justice, and to love kindness, and to walk humbly with your God?" (Micah 6:8). It's the old story. Human life flourishes if and when we are surrounded by a community in which we give and receive care. Life is reciprocal. Justice is received when justice is done. Kindness is earned when kindness is extended. This is not always evident immediately. But eventually the truth endures. So, "let love be genuine" (Romans 12:9).

There is not an instance in time or a place on earth where discipleship does not apply. Discipleship is a lifestyle. It reaches into every home, into every relationship, into every vocation, into every aspect of learning. It challenges our expressions of sexuality, our life of leisure, our world of sport, our saving and spending. God is all in all. Therefore, "present yourselves to God as those who have been brought from death to life, and present your members to God as instruments of righteousness" (Romans 6:13b).

Questions for Discussion

1. What is the Christian's motivation for a life of discipleship?
2. Is Jesus' invitation to discipleship an "impossible ideal" or is it achievable? (See Luke 9:57–58). How is it possible to keep from despairing?
3. Explain how following Christ can be understood as a participation in salvation.
4. What are some influences in society that distract us from the call to discipleship today?
5. Do you respond to Micah 6:8 with joy, or do you feel the call to justice, kindness and humility as a burden? Share practical ways in which Micah 6:8 comes alive in your life.

Christian Spirituality

How can I feel close to God? How is the Holy Spirit present in my life? How do I experience spiritual vitality? These are questions each of us asks from time to time, and at different stages along our journey of faith. How do we understand spiritual life in a Mennonite perspective?

We believe that to be a disciple of Jesus is to know life in the Spirit. Sitting close to God does not necessarily happen by gaining greater distance from the earth. To be sure, there needs to be a distancing from attachment to earthly things. And at the end of life when we face death and anticipate eternal life with God, we will be separated from the earthly existence we have come to know. But while in this life, we should not think that a relationship with God can be achieved most successfully if and when we distance ourselves from our social and natural environment.

For the first disciples, as for disciples today, the context of Christian spirituality is the nitty- gritty of everyday life. The road to spirituality was modeled by Jesus. He led the disciples along the dusty pathways of Palestine and involved them in life's joys and sorrows. There are appropriate times for withdrawal to places of reflection and prayer. But our everyday walk which we describe as Christian discipleship also belongs to our expression of Christian spirituality.

Life in the Spirit is life. It is life lived in the spirit of Jesus Christ. In the Beatitudes which introduce the Sermon on the Mount (Matthew 5:1–12), Jesus pointed to such real-life experiences as poverty (v. 3), suffering (v. 4), thirst (v. 5), peacemaking (v. 9) and cross-bearing (v. 11–12) as connectors to a sense of God's blessing. Blessed are those who live in this way. They experience the closeness of God. Spiritual life and earthly life are intertwined in these ways.

As we experience relationship with God, the life, death and resurrection of Jesus Christ take shape in us and we grow in the image of Christ. Life in the Spirit requires a certain distancing from earthly life, a dying to self. Distance is necessary because "no one can serve two masters" (Matthew 6:24). To grasp our obligation on earth in the right way requires that we not grasp (worship) anything earthly. The Bible speaks of this temptation in terms of flesh. Flesh symbolizes the inclination in each person to invite seeds of corruption into our life. We don't need to look far to understand what is meant here. Over-eating and sexual indulgences are two obvious examples. To maintain a close relationship with God it is necessary to do battle with the flesh.

Flesh is opposed to Spirit. The apostle Paul says to the Galatians: "Live by the Spirit, I say, and do not gratify the desires of the flesh. For what the flesh desires is opposed to the Spirit, and what the Spirit desires is opposed to the flesh" (Galatians 5:16–17). To live by the Spirit means, in simplest words, to open ourselves to the leading of God. This involves the element of death—death to things and death to self.

But this way of life also promises resurrection. A seed will not sprout and become a plant unless it is first buried in the ground. Menno Simons spoke of the Christian life as a "walking in the resurrection." He understood this as a daily experience of spiritual renewal.

By confessing Christ and receiving baptism, we are brought into a new relationship with God through Christ. Christian character forms in a process of decision-making and exercise. We come to a fork in the road and decide upon a life-changing direction. When we exercise the discipline of prayer on a regular basis, our spiritual life is toned much like our muscles are toned through physical exercise. Whether dramatically or gradually, our relationship with Christ takes shape over time. The apostle Paul said: "Train yourself in godliness, for, while physical training is of some value, godliness is valuable in every way, holding promise for both the present life and the life to come" (1 Timothy 4:7b–8).

Life in the Spirit has a beginning and a continuation. After the important experiences and impressions accumulated in childhood, a crucial "rite of passage" occurs, usually during youth. I refer to the public testimony—expressed in the personal act of confessing Christ and receiving baptism—that gives witness to my decision to enter into a maturing spiritual relationship with God through Jesus Christ.

Spiritual growth toward maturity can be expressed in three words. The first word is *freedom*. Through repentance and the claim of forgiveness, we are free from sin and are free to move in a new direction. The congregation bears witness to our stance and gives its blessing to the direction we have chosen. The church provides a freeing context for the exercise of our new relationship with God.

> Now the Lord is the Spirit, and where the Spirit of the Lord is, there is freedom. And all of us . . . are being transformed into the same image from one degree of glory to another; for this comes from the Lord, the Spirit (2 Corinthians 3:17–18).

The second word is h*umility*. Having confessed our humility before God in a spirit of servitude, we are open to the nurture of the Holy Spirit. We have left our quest for power and ego behind. We have submitted to the way of the cross in accordance with Christ who humbled himself and became obedient.

> He will transform the body of our humiliation that it may be conformed to the body of his glory, by the power that also enables him to make all things subject to himself (Philippians 3:21).

The third word is *love*. Having confessed our love for God in a spirit of devotion and cooperation, we make a commitment to rely completely on the Holy Spirit who nurtures us in community and affords us an opportunity to nurture others.

> Speaking the truth in love, we must grow up in every way into him who is the head, into Christ, from whom the whole body, joined and knit together by every ligament with which it is equipped, as each part is working properly, promotes the body's growth by building itself up in love (Ephesians 4:15–16).

We draw the life of the Spirit from Jesus Christ, just as a branch draws life from the vine. To continue spiritual life once it has begun, we are given the gift of community. Spiritual community has two dimensions: Christ and the church of Christ. The two are inseparable. You can't have one without the other. Both are necessary for Christian spirituality to flourish in and among us. The intimacy of these two dimensions is reflected in the statement that "we are to grow up in every way into Christ, who is the head of the church, through whom it is built up in love" (*Confession of Faith in a Mennonite Perspective,* 69).

In John's Gospel we find a picture of spiritual life drawn with vines and branches. It is a picture of our bond with Christ and our communal relationship with each other.

> I am the vine, you are the branches. Those who abide in me and I in them bear much fruit, because apart from me you can do nothing. . . . If you abide in me, and my words abide in you, ask for whatever you wish, and it will be done for you. My Father is glorified by this, that you bear much fruit and become my disciples (John 15:5,7–8).

The relationship of Christ with his disciples is woven into an inseparable intimacy in this picture. This intimacy speaks of a togetherness as intertwined as life and breath itself.

The fruit of the Spirit evidenced in community is "love, joy, peace, patience, kindness, generosity, faithfulness, gentleness, and self-control" (Galatians 5:22). These virtues, promised for followers of Christ, characterize the works and attitude of Christ himself. By our response to these promises we can tell the difference between a genuine and a false claim to spirituality. If a person claims to be filled with the Holy Spirit, and the manifestation of the Spirit agrees with what we know about Jesus Christ, then the claim is valid. If a person's life does not match, however incompletely, with what we know of Jesus, then the claim is doubtful.

Spiritual disciplines such as prayer, study of Scripture, reflection on God, corporate worship, singing hymns, simplicity, witness and service are training in godliness. Prayer is communication with God. Prayer can be uttered in words or groanings. Prayer can also occur unexpressed. It is said of some persons that they live a life of prayer. Prayer is to spiritual life like breathing is to physical life.

The study of Scripture is an essential spiritual discipline. There is a temptation in our day to read anything and everything but the Bible. The Bible is the Christian's main reading material. The Scriptures are inexhaustible in their understanding and application. One is never through with reading the Bible. Committing great passages of the Bible to memory is a helpful discipline. That way biblical passages become a source for meditation at any time.

Individual and communal worship provide time and space for reflection on God. Praise and thanksgiving keep us alive to God and give us perspective on the source and goal of life. Singing and hearing a wide range of religious music edifies the soul. This includes hymns, classical anthems, spiritual folk songs and also wordless music.

The simple life is cherished particularly by some groups in the Mennonite family. Their example is instructive to us all. In a world of technology, life becomes increasingly complex and we become more and more preoccupied with efficient ways of conquering time and space. Also, we cultivate a false sense of power and invincibility. This can lead us away from sensitivity to God's touch. We need to become aware of this trend in modern society. We need to claim a lifestyle that allows God to touch our lives in simple ways.

The Mennonite church offers opportunities for young and old to serve others in the name of Christ. Christian service is a medium of Christian spirituality. Spiritual nurture needs to occur in a context which provides for the ebb and flow of quiet meditation and active service.

Nothing can separate us from the love of God in Christ Jesus our Lord, for God can use both joy and suffering to nurture our spiritual growth. There is no magic short-cut to Christian spirituality. Indeed, the pathway to joy is often fraught with suffering. Meanwhile, the most important thing we need to know about our spiritual state is that God loves us tenaciously and eternally. "For I am convinced that neither death, nor life, nor angels, nor rulers, nor things present, nor things to come, nor powers, nor height, nor depth, nor anything else in all creation, will be able to separate us from the love of God in Christ Jesus our Lord" (Romans 8:38–39).

Questions for Discussion

1. To be spiritual is to be close to God. How does following Christ in life contribute to our spirituality? (See *Confession,* page 70, note 1.)
2. Spiritual life requires the discipline of leaving behind the things that hinder the Christian walk. Share successes and failures you have experienced in this regard.
3. How is spiritual discipline like physical exercise? Which spiritual exercises (page 108 and your additions) do you find helpful?
4. The Bible emphasizes the connection between spiritual growth and life in community. What spiritual good can come from participation in Christian community?

A genuine Christian faith cannot be idle,
  but it changes, renews, purifies, sanctifies, and
    justifies more and more.
It gives peace and joy, for by faith
  it knows that hell, the devil, sin, and death
    are conquered through Christ,
  and that grace, mercy, pardon from sin,
    and eternal life are acquired through Him.
In full confidence
  it approaches the Father in the name of Christ,
  receives the Holy Ghost,
  becomes partaker in the divine nature,
  and is renewed after the image of Him
    who created him.
It lives out of the power of Christ
  which is in it;
all its ways are righteousness, godliness,
  honesty, chastity, truth, wisdom,
  goodness, kindness, light, love, peace.
                              —Menno Simons

Family, Singleness, and Marriage

Is the family a sacred institution? Or is the family a throw-away commodity? Today the family as we have known it tradition-ally is under seige. Will it survivie? What is the biblical way to think about families and about the related aspects of singleness and marriage? How can we live the biblical way?

We believe that God intends human life to begin in families. God has created us in families. This was so in the beginning when the Creator fashioned humankind in a community of man and woman (Genesis 1:27). It is evident today that this family unit held the potential of spawning a human family numbering in the billions. Thus the Lord's command has been followed: "Be fruitful and multiply and fill the earth . . ." (1:28). God intended life to produce a numberless human family, and it did.

Families come in many shapes and sizes. We speak of the nuclear family, where mother and father and children live together under one roof. There is the intergenerational family, which includes grandparents and even great-grandparents. We refer as well to the extended family. This includes brothers and sisters, aunts and uncles, cousins, nieces and nephews. It is good to think of family in such a broader circle, which can include those married and those not married.

The nuclear family, the intergenerational family and the extended family are linked biologically and culturally. So is the genealogical family, which includes generations of relatives, living as well as deceased. Biologically speaking, the entire human race comprised of all peoples of this earth is one human family. The pattern of family life established with the original creation provides a wonderful opportunity for persons to inherit and to foster the secure surroundings of family relationships and also to identify with all peoples of the earth as our sisters and brothers.

We admit with regret that while God's original intention for families is still in evidence, not all is well with the human family in our day. Too often newborn infants are not afforded the privilege of beginning their life in families. A significant number of children do not enjoy the benefit and blessing of protective family life. An alarming number of persons in their teens and early adulthood experience dysfunctional family relationships. Marital relationships among adults are often strained, contributing to family breakdown. A growing number of elderly persons are left alone and without family care in their later years. For many, life does not begin or end in families. Nor is it sustained by family life. But this is not the end of the story.

God intends human life to be blessed through families. The Scriptures call us to surround the biological family with the family of faith. First man and first woman were created by God with the expectation that they would turn their attention to God. Their relationship was proscribed not only biologically but also by faith. The same was true of the family of Abraham and Sarah. The Lord God laid a claim upon the future generations of their family with the promise, "in you all the families of the earth will be blessed" (Genesis 12:3). They were to be a people of God through whom all families (nations and races) of the earth would be blessed spiritually. The divine foundation of the family is evident in such texts as Psalm 27:10: "If my father and mother forsake me, the Lord will take me up."

The church is a family, a family of faith. The church has inherited the blessing given by the Lord God to the family of Abraham and Sarah, the blessing of salvation in Jesus Christ. The apostle Peter proclaimed: "You are the descendants of the prophets and of the covenant that God gave to your ancestors, saying to Abraham, 'And in your descendants all the families of the earth shall be blessed'" (Acts.3:25).

The Ephesian Christians, a diverse group including persons of Jewish and of Gentile background, are encouraged to nonetheless become a family of faith: "So then you are no longer strangers and aliens, but you are citizens with the saints and also members of the household of God" (Ephesians 2:19).

Jesus set the stage for an expansion of the family system beyond its biological circle. As a youth he distanced himself from his parents to indicate that he gave primary loyalty to his heavenly Father. To his parents who found him in the temple he said: "Did you not know that I must be in my Father's house?" (Luke 2:49). During his ministry, when someone inquired about his biological family, he said: "My mother and my brothers are those who hear the word of God and do it" (Luke 8:21).

This paves the way for the church family. The church family is a channel of blessing to all nations and races of the world. Today the church is dispersed throughout the world and draws its membership from all peoples of the earth. The church family is a spiritual home into which everyone is invited and through which each and all can be blessed.

While life begins in families, not everyone needs to marry. Within the church family, the goodness of being single or married is respected. "So then, he who marries his fiancée does well; and he who refrains from marriage will do well" (1 Corinthians 7:38). Single persons—those who have never married or those who were married at one time—can belong to the church family and participate fully in its life. While the church includes and serves biological families, the larger reality giving definition and shape to the church's self-understanding and ministry is the spiritual family. The apostle Paul commends voluntary singleness as an opportunity for heightened commitment to the work of the Lord (1 Corinthians 7:25–35).

We believe that God intended marriage to be a covenant between one man and one woman for life. Marriage has its rightful place in God's intended order. While there is no one place in the Bible that spells out a full theology of marriage, the following summarizes the biblical order for marriage: 1) Marriage is a covenant between one man and one woman (Genesis 2:24). 2) Marriage is for as long as life shall last (Mark 10:9). 3) Marriage is a relationship of mutual submission to Christ (Ephesians 5:21). 4) Marriage is a covenant made in the context of the church. 5) Sexual union is meant only for the marriage relationship (Exodus 20:14). 6) Marriage is meant for sexual intimacy, companionship, the birth and nurture of children, and for building a social unit that reflects faith in God.

Children are of great importance. Jesus saw them as examples of how to receive the reign of God. People who cannot stand up for their rights in a society or who have no one to advocate on their behalf are always in danger of becoming downtrodden and neglected. This happens to children from time to time. Thus it is noteworthy when the importance of children is upheld by influential people. The Israelites were instructed by the Lord to respect and care for the children in their midst. Even then there was a tendency to favour the firstborn above the others and to favour male children above females.

In societies surrounding Palestine in New Testament times, negative attitudes toward children were common. Historians tell of the practice of infanticide (causing infants to die) directed particularly at unwanted females. One day, when Jesus observed a negative attitude toward children, he used the occasion to point to the value of little ones (Mark 10:13–16). He endorsed the practice of blessing children.

He also pointed to children as a sign of how adults should receive the kingdom of God. Just like the children came to Jesus in trust and without fear, so adults should receive God's kingdom. He said, "Whoever does not receive the kingdom of God as a little child will never enter it" (Mark 10:15). Jesus' gesture and his words paved the way for the Christian congregation's love and care for the children in its midst.

While children need to be respected, they also need to be taught respect for others. One of the Ten Commandments promises that if children honour their parents, it will go well with them in the land (Exodus 20:12). Here the principle applies that if you show respect for your parents, your children will show respect for you. The same principle applies in the church family. Thus the apostle Paul instructs Timothy: "Do not speak harshly to an older man, but speak to him as to a father, to younger men as brothers, to older women as mothers, to younger women as sisters—with absolute purity" (1 Timothy 5:1–2). How you treat persons in your generation will show up in the way persons act in the next generation.

As the family of God, the church is called to be a sanctuary offering hope and healing for families. It was mentioned earlier in this chapter that not all is well in modern family life. Indeed some speak of a crisis in the family in our time. There are many contributing factors, including a general turning to violence to deal with issues, a weakening of the sense of responsibility, an unwillingness to work at relationships when difficulties arise, social pressures coming from secular life-styles, economic pressures, and other factors.

The crisis of the family is felt in the church. The breakdown of marriage and family occurs within the church family as well. It belongs to the agenda of the church to work with this problem. We are inspired by the vision of hope and healing. Our ministry is based on the confession that "God who reconciled us to himself through Christ . . . has given us the ministry of reconciliation" (2 Corinthians 5:18).

We live in a broken world, a world in which not all things can be fixed as we would like. At the same time, we believe in the power of the resurrection, a power that can do amazing things in our midst. The church is a sanctuary of safety and hope in which God can heal broken relationships through our caring ministries.

Questions for Discussion

1. Read the five statements of belief highlighted in this chapter. Discuss the practical implications of each statement.
2. Family includes more than the nuclear family. How much more?
3. Singleness is commended by the apostle Paul as an opportunity for heightened commitment to the Lord (1 Corinthians 7:25–35). What do you think of this view? What is the church's responsibility to singles?
4. Why should we "bend over backwards" to protect, nurture and "hear" the children in our midst?
5. In what ways can the church be a sanctuary of healing and hope for families in our time?

Truth and the Avoidance of Oaths

Mennonites seek to follow the teachings of the Jesus. One of these teachings, found in the Sermon on the Mount, concerns the swearing of oaths. We read: "Do not swear at all. . . . Let your word be 'Yes, Yes' or 'No, No'; anything more than that comes from the evil one" (Matthew 5:34,37). The apostle James repeats and supports this teaching with his admonition: "Above all, my beloved, do not swear, either by heaven or by earth or by any other oath, but let your 'Yes' be yes and your 'No' be no, so that you may not fall under condemnation" (James 5:12).

This commandment has been and still is practised by Mennonites when they are asked to make an oath in court. The usual practice in society is to place your hand on the Bible, and say, "I swear to tell the truth, the whole truth, and nothing but the truth." This gesture reminds the person being questioned of the seriousness of what he or she says. You had better speak the truth, for you speak under oath! Your words can be held against you.

Mennonites have historically opted out of this requirement. Following the teaching of Jesus, they have chosen not to swear by the Bible. Rather, they say: "I choose to affirm that I will speak the truth." This alternative is allowed, by law. The insistence to affirm rather than swear is a sign of the hesitation Mennonites have expressed historically in regard to involvements with the courts. Ideally, the church provides the context where matters are settled. But today's Mennonites do not live in this ideal world.

The matter of confirming with a simple yes or no, rather than swearing on the Bible, is only one aspect of a wider issue. Jesus teaches that there is no need to bolster promises or statements of truth with oaths. A person should simply speak the truth. Otherwise your hearers can assume that occasionally (or normally?), when it is convenient, you would not be truthful.

We commit ourselves to tell the truth, to give a simple yes or no, and to avoid swearing of oaths. Faithfulness is a vital character trait of the Christian. But how is faithfulness expressed? How do people observe faithfulness and assess it? The answer is simple. Faithfulness is measured by whether we stand behind the words we speak; whether we keep the promises we make. Words must not become idle talk. Promises are not made to be broken. When we speak words that are believable and make promises that can be trusted, our life points with integrity to the One whose life we claim to image.

The Old Testament community was quite involved in stating promises and making formal agreements. Their commitments were called covenants. Covenant-making became quite formal. The ritual included signs which lent seriousness to the promise. For example, when the Lord promised land and generations of children to Abraham (Genesis 7), male circumcision was the sign of the covenant (17:9–14, 23–27). Down through the generations, circumcision became a permanent and ever-recurring reminder of the covenant God had made with Abraham and his offspring.

A vow made to the Lord or to another person was sometimes fortified by "swearing an oath." The oath was a backup to the covenant. A person buying a piece of land might promise to complete the payment within five years. To back up his promise he might say, "I swear to God to keep my promise." Or, "May God strike me dead if I fail to keep my promise to you." This was an attempt to add weight to the promise.

It appears not to have been wrong to make oaths in this way. Still the important thing was to keep the original spoken promise. Sometimes the oath served as a cover-up for the weakness of the promise. That is why the reminder: "When a man makes a vow to the Lord, or swears an oath to bind himself by a pledge, he shall not break his word; he shall do according to all that proceeds out of his mouth" (Numbers 30:2). Keeping the original promise made is what matters in covenant making.

Jesus told his disciples not to swear oaths at all, but to let there yes be yes, and their no be no. Jesus focused attention on living the truth. He blessed "the pure in heart" (Matthew 6:8), the persons who exuded singular devotion to God. What they say and do in life has a direct correlation with God's will. He criticized those who say, "Lord, Lord," but do not follow through with doing the will of God (7:21). He wanted people not only to hear his words, but also to act on them. He illustrated his point by comparing a house built on sand with a house built on a rock (7:24–27). Jesus called for people to live the truth of God with integrity.

This emphasis is in keeping with Jesus' words against swearing of oaths. For one thing, if what you say and the way you live is an open book, it is unnecessary to add a word of fortification to your promise. When people ask the question about what is involved in following Jesus, they should know that what they see is what it's all about. In the same spirit, a simple yes or no should say it all. No further defence is needed. It's simply a matter of speaking the truth in love (Ephesians 4:15), and in this way "your words may give grace to those who hear" (4:29).

It sounds almost too simple. But the principle for life relationships is contained in this rule: "Owe no one anything but to love one another, for the one who loves another has fulfilled the law" (Romans 13:8). This principle supports the point that our communication with one another should be straightforward and truthful. Yes means yes, and no means no. These words, spoken by persons who claim to believe in and rely on a faithful God, are sacred and binding.

Jesus warned against using oaths to try to compel God to guarantee the future. Jesus took the matter one step further. He said to his followers, "Do not swear at all" (Matthew 5:34). He meant, we should not add an additional guarantee to our vow. More specifically, we should not invoke anything in God's creation as a gamble or wager as to how things would turn out. "But I say to you, Do not swear at all, either by heaven, for it is the throne of God, or by the earth, for it is his footstool, or by Jerusalem, for it is the city of the great King. And do not swear by your head, for you cannot make one hair white or black" (5:34–35). To do so puts God to the test, which we must not do. Furthermore, in so doing we avoid facing our own responsibilities.

To invoke God in this risky way was particularly tempting to the scribes and Pharisees. They already assumed they had the edge on knowing how God operates. With this inner knowledge, they presumed they could use their religion freely to fortify their vows. In this way they profane or secularize the name of God (Leviticus 19:11–12). That is, they try to bring God down to an earthly level.

Jesus speaks harshly against this way of selectively "swearing" your way through a situation (Matthew 23:16–22). He tells the Pharisees they have no right to decide what is sacred and what is not. Thus they have no basis on which to determine what is valid to swear by and what is not. They must not put God to the test in order to serve their own purposes of having things turn out the way they would wish. The practice of swearing oaths had gotten woefully out of hand. The practice of "telling it like it is" had been lost.

As Christians, our first allegiance is to God. In our modern day, as in all times, the habit of taking the name of the Lord in vain (swearing) is all too common. People who are not attuned to the holiness of God and the special place that divine names have in worship use words like "God" and "Jesus Christ" freely in connection with profane speech. Often these names are invoked to express frustration and anger in a situation.

Christians have no desire or need to talk in this way. Such talk is profanity, which reduces the sacred to the profane, the heavenly to the earthly. It should be painful to Christians when they hear this use of biblical language. In contrast, the believers' use of names for God and for Jesus Christ engenders a spirit of warmth and devotion. Our use of divine names indicates a singular allegiance to God. The wisdom of Proverbs guides our sentiments: "Incline your ear and hear my words, and apply your mind to my teaching; for it will be pleasant if you keep them within you, if all of them are ready on your lips. So that your trust may be in the Lord, I have made them known to you today— yes, to you" (Proverbs 22:17–19).

We find ourselves in a society which affords numerous subtle and not so subtle opportunities for expressing oaths of allegiance. Political parties within our country invite our allegiance, as does the country as such, particularly in times of war. Traditional secret societies sometimes require oaths of their members which hinge on life and death. Fraternities and street gangs sometimes call for an oath of loyalty. Peer groups exert subtle power on the lifestyle of their adherents.

The church nurtures the believers' allegiance to God alone. While the church is a free society, inviting all to join and constraining no one to remain a member, there is an expectation that persons will take their promise of membership seriously. Yet the purpose of commitment to the body of Christ is to free people to express their loyalty in grace and truth. The Holy Spirit works in and through the community of faith to free people from subversion to oaths by encouraging them to speak and live in truthfulness before God and all people.

Questions for Discussion

1. What is the main emphasis of each of the following texts: Matthew 5:33–37; James 5:12; Ephesians 4:15, 29; Acts 5:29?

2. Why do Mennonites consider it wrong to swear an oath?
3. What are the risks in living as "an open book" (page 119) in the community of faith and in the world?
4. What are the consequences of habitually telling only half the truth, or of lying persistently?
5. Explore the rich implications of Proverbs 22:17–19.

21

Christian Stewardship

The practice of Christian stewardship should be of great interest to us. We live and work in a context where it is possible to accumulate great amounts of wealth. Many members of our congregations are wealthy. Individually and together we are rich in material resources, especially when compared to the majority of people on earth. How shall we live as faithful Christian stewards?

We believe that everything belongs to God who calls us, as the church, to live as faithful stewards of all that God has entrusted to us. In biblical times managers or stewards were appointed to take charge of sectors of societal or business life. For example, a steward might have the assignment of managing a vineyard. Tasks would include setting up schedules, ordering materials, giving a financial account of earnings and spendings, attending to human relations, paying wages, assessing work accomplished, and much more. We can compare the steward of biblical times with the assignment given to a person in a managerial role in modern times.

Jesus tells the parable about the steward of a household, left in charge by the owner. The parable begins: "Who then is the wise and faithful steward whom his master will put in charge of his servants to give them their allowance of food at the proper time?" (Luke 12:42) In this parable the steward is manager of the food supply. The manager stocks the food pantry, oversees the quality and holds the key to the kitchen. The steward is responsible to see that this part of the master's household is properly cared for.

In the New Testament, stewardship also applies to responsibilities in the church. In Titus 1:7, the overseer or bishop of the

Christian stewardship is
a person's grateful obedient response to
God's redeeming love
expressed through
the use of all our resources
for the continuation of
God's mission in the world.
—Daniel Kauffman

church is called a steward. In 1 Corinthians 4:1 Paul speaks of himself as a steward of the gospel. And in Ephesians 3:2 the apostle depicts himself as a steward of the grace of God. In 1 Peter 4:10–11 the entire church community has a stewardship to fulfil with whatever gift God has given, whether in speaking or in service.

In this application of the term "steward," the assignment is at times an official task. At other times the term is used functionally to speak of the informal obligation of the Christian to exercise gifts and talents given by God. Each believer has the responsibility and privilege to exercise his or her stewardship with the available time and talents and opportunities.

As servants of God, our primary vocation is to be faithful stewards of God's household. As God's managers, our collective responsibility covers at least five overlapping areas: talents, time, things (including money), the earth (the environment) and the Gospel.

In today's language, *talents* refer to personal abilities. We say: "You have a talent for playing piano," or, "You are talented in woodworking." But biblically speaking the definition is broader. Talents are gifts which God places in our hands. Talents come in various ways and various forms. A situation into which we are placed and which affords us opportunity to express God's love and care is a talent in our hands. The gift of patience in a situation which needs special attention is a special talent which befalls some people. The inheritance of family security is a talent in our hands. In the broadest sense, "everything you have and everything you are comprises the talent entrusted to you by God" (Robert Vallet).

Risk is required to bring our talents to an effective level. If we are too calculating, too preservative, the gifts we hold in hand will not reach their intended goal. This is the point of Jesus' parable of the talents (Matthew 25:14–30). A property owner entrusted his investments ("talents") to servants. Upon his return he asked the servants to give account. Two had invested well their talents, but one had only hidden the talent. The master had hard words for this one who had no vision of the ripple effect a talent could create. The words of 1 Peter 4:10 apply here: "As good stewards serve one another with whatever gift each of you has received."

We believe that time belongs to God and that we are to use with care the time of which we are stewards. *Time* is one of God's gifts to us. We are stewards of God's time. The Psalmist says: "My times are in your hands" (31:15). The lesson for us is obvious: "Be careful then how you live, not as unwise people but as wise, making the most of the time, because the days are evil" (Ephesians 5:15–16). Time is no throw-away commodity to be used and abused as we wish. We live in and on God's time. God is our beginning (Alpha) and our end (Omega), two points of reference that form the divine parentheses for your life and mine.

By example, the Creator taught a wise lesson about the use of time. After working for six days, the Lord God rested on the seventh day. In keeping with this example, each seventh day of our existence is declared a day of rest: "Remember the sabbath day, and keep it holy. Six days you shall labour and do all your work. But the seventh day is a sabbath to the Lord your God; you shall not do any work . . ." (Exodus 20:8–10). After Israel's deliverance from slavery in Egypt, the sabbath day was celebrated in remembrance of God's miraculous rescue. It was a day set aside to praise God for salvation. For the Christian church, the sabbath day is celebrated each Sunday, the Christian day of salvation, the day of Christ's resurrection from the dead.

Jesus observed that the sabbath law was stifling the intent of God's redemption. Surely one should save life—including animals—from trouble even on the sabbath. "The sabbath was made for humankind, and not humankind for the sabbath"

(Mark 2:27). In stating that "the Son of Man is lord even of the sabbath" (2:28), Jesus hallowed (set apart) all time for doing justice, for proclaiming salvation and for the ministry of healing.

We acknowledge that God as Creator is owner of all things. *Things* have been given into our hands for responsible use. This includes our so-called possessions, our money, and the real estate that we claim to own.

Money and possessions have incredible power over us. During the mid-1800s the French historian, Alexis DeTocqueville, sought to capture the spirit of the American dream. Travelling about in the United States, he took notes on his impressions of people in America. In one comment he concluded: "I know of no other country where the love of money has taken stronger hold on the affections of men."

Some people get so wrapped up in their money that they would rather die than part with it. People will put their life at risk to defend their property and their possessions. In the parable of the rich fool (Luke 12:13–21), God tells the rich man in the end: "You fool! This very night your life is being demanded of you. And the things you have prepared, whose will they be?" (12:20).

Why not share money and possessions with those who are in need of it? God created the world so there would be a balance between abundance and need. The apostle Paul appeals to this principle when he asks for funds from the Corinthian Christians to help poor people in other places: ". . . it is a question of a fair balance between your present abundance and their need, so that their abundance may be for your need, in order that there might be a fair balance" (2 Corinthians 8:13b–14).

The key to a generous attitude is to "keep your lives free from the love of money, and be content with what you have" (Hebrews 13:5). Remember as well that a vibrant church is a giving church. Generosity reflects the gift of salvation that our

Lord so generously lavished upon us all (2 Corinthians 8:9).

It is not only a matter of balance or of generosity. Justice is at stake. A Christian conscience cannot rest when some people live in lavish houses and eat sumptuously while others huddle in meagre huts and go hungry. Do the words of the apostle James apply to this situation? "Listen! The wages of the laborers who mowed your fields, which you kept back by fraud, cry out, and the cries of the harvesters have reached the ears of the Lord of hosts" (James 5:4). Money and possessions raise issues of justice.

As stewards of God's earth, we are called to care for the earth and to bring rest and renewal to the land and everything that lives on it. The basis for Christian stewardship of *the earth* is laid in the first chapter of the Bible. There it is assumed that the Lord God is the owner of the universe. Since God created the world and all that is in it, all belongs to the Creator. This assumption is indicated in the Levitical law: "The land shall not be sold in perpetuity, for the land is mine; with me you are but aliens and tenants" (Leviticus 25:23). This is reiterated in Psalm 24:1: "The earth is the Lord's and all that is in it, the world, and those who live in it."

Stewardship is a useful concept for picturing our relationship to God relative to creation and to redemption. The steward is not the owner of the household but the manager who lives in the owner's house and manages a part of the household. We are accountable to God for the way we treat life. We regard ourselves as servants of one another, not as masters over each other. We relate to people and to things in a servile way, placing ourselves on the same level relative to all people. We look to God as our redeemer, and we point others to God for salvation. In the end our reward is to hear the words: "Well done, good and trustworthy slave; you have been trustworthy in a few things, I will put you in charge of many things; enter into the joy of your master" (Matthew 25:21).

It is awesome to think that God is the owner of this vast piece of real estate called the universe. It is just as impressive to realize that humans—you and I—were given the privilege of co-managing the created world with God. What an assignment! "God said, 'See, I have given you every plant yielding seed . . . and every tree. . . and every beast of the earth . . . everything that has the breath of life. . . .' And it was so" (Genesis 1:29–30). The agreement is that humankind will care for the resources of the universe in a sharing mode.

Jesus showed a practical way of implementing justice upon earth. He appealed to the Israelite practice of the Jubilee year. In the seven-times-seventh year or the fiftieth year Israel announced rest and freedom for the land and for its workers. Family land was returned, debts were forgiven and slaves were freed. A new beginning was afforded people who were mired in obligations that bound them. This was a way of extending generosity from the "haves" to the "have nots." It was a sign of the kingdom of God.

We are called to be stewards in the household of God, set apart for the service of God. Every believer is a steward of *the gospel.* Each of us has the responsibility to share God's love with those we see and touch from day to day. We are to think of ourselves as "servants of Christ and stewards of God's mysteries" (1 Corinthians 4:1).

Leaders in the Christian community have a special obligation by virtue of their public promise to serve the church in the name of Christ (Titus 1:7). Leaders are to teach sound doctrine, in this way exercising faithful stewardship of the gospel entrusted to them (2:1). All in the church, older and younger, men and women, are to take the stewardship of the gospel seriously (2:2–10). Stewardship is the responsibility of the entire Christian community.

Questions for Discussion

1. Read the six statements of belief found in bold print in this chapter. Then give a one-sentence definition of Christian stewardship.
2. After reading the section on talents (pages 125–126), identify your talents and the talents of others in your study group. How can we help each other in being good stewards of these talents?
3. Where do you experience success and failure in managing time?
4. The greatest difficulty in living as faithful stewards seems to centre on material possessions or things. Study Matthew 6:24–33 and the parable of Luke 12:13–21. What temptations and challenges face you as a Christian in this area?
5. God is owner of the universe; we are co-managers with God. How does this belief inform your Christian life?

Peace, Justice, and Nonresistance

The Mennonite church considers itself a steward of the gospel of peace. Practically every one of the many Confessions of Faith accepted by Mennonites over the centuries of their history speaks against taking revenge and against military service. Mennonites are part of what is known as the "historic peace churches." These church groups uphold the pacifist position. To this group belong the Society of Friends (Quakers), the Brethren in Christ, the Church of the Brethren, the Hutterites and the Amish. Besides these churches, there are countless Christians who accept the peace position as part of their understanding of the Gospel. What do we believe about peace?

We believe that peace is the will of God. The Creator wove the message of peace into the creation of the universe. Each element of the natural environment fits into a supportive pattern. Humans were placed in the centre of God's creation. Their calling, together with the rest of creation, was to be fruitful and multiply and fill the earth. The operative words are "good," not evil, and "flourish," not destroy. This implies a peaceful environment where justice can flourish.

Original creation featured a universe in which humans were given the key to peaceable life on earth. They should rely on the Lord God for their knowledge of what was right (good) and wrong (evil) rather than cut themselves off from God and rely on their own humanly concocted ideas. This was the meaning of the tree of the knowledge of good and evil from which Adam and Eve were forbidden to eat. They should look to God as the author and finisher of life rather than take life into their own hands. This was the meaning of the tree of life which Adam and Eve were to respect.

Although God created a peaceable world, humanity chose the way of unrighteousness and violence. Our first parents chose the selfish way, their own way. They placed their trust in themselves rather than in God. Thus they embarked on the slippery slope which leads from self-assertion (egoism) to self-worship (playing "god"). This was evident in what Cain did to Abel and in the behaviour of the people during the time of Noah. Our sinful inclination is to do the same.

All the while, God was gracious and purposeful. Adam and Eve were driven from the Garden as a measure of protection from their folly (Genesis 3). Cain was sent to the land of Nod after he killed his brother Abel. There he was protected from the vengeance sought by those who would remember his crime (Genesis 4). Because Noah pleased God, he and his family were rescued from the wicked society in which he lived (Genesis 6–9). It was God's plan not to let violence spiral and get out of hand on the human scene.

The children of Israel heard the clear promise of peace. The Lord God said: "I will grant peace in the land, and you shall lie down, and no one shall make you afraid; I will remove dangerous animals from the land, and no sword shall go through your land" (Leviticus 26:6). The prophet Isaiah saw the vision of a peaceable kingdom where the people "shall beat their swords into ploughshares, and their spears into pruning hooks; nation shall not lift up sword against nation, neither shall they learn war anymore" (Isaiah 2:4). Hosea's prophetic vision included this word from the Lord: "I will abolish the bow, the sword, and war from the land; and I will make you lie down in safety" (Hosea 2:18).

After thousands of years, we still aspire to the way of peace and justice. Our hopes and aspirations are not different from the Old Testament people. We want to live in safety in our local and worldwide communities. We want to worship in freedom. We want to be treated fairly by those in authority. God also wants this for all people. Justice and peace are the will of God.

We do not require anyone
  to shed his blood for us.
We would rather
  die ourselves
    or languish in prison
    or leave our homes
  and settle again in some wilderness
    as our forebears have done
  than to require
    a sacrifice of any kind
    by anyone on our behalf.
                          —David Toews
                          November 4, 1918

The peace God which intends for humanity and creation was revealed most fully in Jesus Christ. The promise of peace and justice became evident in the revelation of God in Jesus Christ. Jesus incarnated God's will for peace and justice. At the announcement of his birth, his mother Mary rejoiced that the child would bring justice to the oppressed (Luke 1:52–53). Zechariah, the father of John the Baptist, prophesied that the child would "guide our feet into the way of peace" (1:79). At Jesus' birth the angels proclaimed the arrival of "peace on earth among those whom he favours" (2:14).

Jesus did not force his way of peace on others. He taught peace and he invited disciples to the way of peace. But for many his teachings were not easy to accept. Some wanted him to take sides—their side. Some wanted an immediately effective solution, a lightning bolt from heaven. Jesus could have done that. When Judas and the soldiers were about to capture him, one of the disciples tried to defend him. Jesus said to him, "Put your sword back into its place; for all who take the sword will perish by the sword. Do you think I cannot appeal to my Father, and he will at once send me more than twelve legions of angels?" (Matthew 26:52–53) He could have provided an instant end to the matter, but he did not. Jesus worked within the situation from below.

At the same time the principles of his way were unmistakable. He set these before his hearers in word and in action. He said: "Love your enemies and pray for those who persecute you" (Matthew 5:44). These words were spoken so that people would reflect on their own responsibilities. His actions have their climax in the steps that led to his death on the cross and in the death itself. His way of suffering is cause for both admiration and for emulation. "Christ also suffered for you, leaving you an example, so that you should follow in his steps" (1 Peter 2:21). The Scripture continues: "He committed no sin, and no deceit was found in his mouth. When he was abused, he did not return abuse; when he suffered, he did not threaten; but he entrusted himself to the one who judges justly" (2:22–23).

The word "sin" in this verse means violence. To cause another person to suffer is to commit a sin. Jesus absorbed the violence that was done against him. In this way he absorbed the sins of his accusors. In suffering as an innocent person in response to abuse, Jesus passed the ultimate expression of nonresistance. In this way of suffering he took the sins of humankind upon himself, and accomplished our salvation: "He himself bore our sins [meaning violence] in his body on the cross, so that, free from sins, we might live for righteousness [meaning justice]; by his wounds you have been healed" (1 Peter 2:24).

Notice how peace and nonresistance and justice combine in Jesus Christ. He responded peacefully and nonviolently to the sin that was hurled against him. In this way he absorbed the sins of humankind in grace and forgiveness. When we receive this grace and participate in his way of peace, we are "saved by this life" (Romans 5:10).

There is another dimension of peace that needs to be noted. The Bible places special emphasis on peace between nations and races. When we read in Ephesians that "he (Jesus) is our peace; in his flesh he has made both groups into one" (2:14), the two groups referred to are the Jews and the Gentiles. These two races were about as far apart as one can imagine racial families to be. Yet they were "brought near [to each other] by the blood of Christ" (2:13). Jesus extended his hand of reconciliation to both peoples in a most impressive gesture of peace. "All this is from God, who reconciled us to himself through Christ, and has given us the ministry of reconciliation; that is, in Christ God was reconciling the world to himself, not counting their trespasses against them, and entrusting the message of reconciliation to us" (2 Corinthians 5:18–19).

As followers of Jesus, we participate in his ministry of peace and justice. You can't have it both ways. You cannot be for war and for peace at the same time. You cannot be a member of the army that sheds blood as well as the army that sheds no blood. You decide to hold a grudge or you decide to forgive. It's either resistance or nonresistance. Jesus' way for us is clear: "So we are ambassadors for Christ, since God is making his appeal through us; we entreat you on behalf of Christ, be reconciled to God. For our sake he made him to be sin who knew no sin, so that in him we might become the righteousness of God" (2 Corinthians 5:20–21).

Led by the Spirit, and beginning in the church, we witness to all people that violence is not the will of God. Peace has a broader application than the question of the army. The title of our chapter includes nonresistance and justice. The scope of concern includes peace in all our relationships. Involvement in war implicates not only soldiers but also citizens who pay taxes. For that reason some Christians refuse to submit to the government that portion of their taxes which supports the war effort. Everyone involved in modern life is faced in some way with the issues of war and peace, resistance and nonresistance, injustice and justice.

Matters of peace should be on the church's agenda at all times. There is constant opportunity to speak to people concerning peace and to act in peaceful ways. This is not an easy road. For that reason the church needs to be united and supportive in its peace witness.

We give our ultimate loyalty to the God of grace and peace. People of peace look in four directions for their encouragement and direction. 1) They look into the past and find a supportive tradition of peacemakers in the Bible and in the history of the church. 2) They look around them and see people living the way of peace. They also see countless needs in the world that cry for the peace witness. 3) They look into the future and see the vision of the peaceable kingdom, as expressed in Isaiah's prophecy: "The wolf shall lie down with the lamb. . . . They shall not hurt or destroy on all my holy mountain; for the earth will be full of the knowledge of the Lord as the waters cover the sea" (Isaiah 11:6a–9). 4) They look to God who is Love.

Questions for Discussion

1. The Mennonite church is a peace church because of the teachings of the Bible. Summarize the biblical basis for our claim that peace belongs to the good news of the gospel.
2. Where do we see God's desire for peace expressed in the Old Testament? Where does Isaiah 2:1–5 fit into the scheme of history and into daily life today?
3. Where do we see God's desire for peace expressed in the New Testament? Explain how Jesus' way of life is a basis for a theology of peace.
4. Explain how peace and justice go hand in hand (Psalm 85:10). Give examples of how this works in everyday situations. Where do you see injustices? How can we address them?
5. How far should we take the stance of nonresistance? Is there a limit to the tolerance of violence?

The Church's Relation to Government and Society

Mennonites believe in the separation of church and state. What does this mean for our faith?

We believe that the church is God's "holy nation," called to give full allegiance to Christ its head and to witness to all nations about God's saving love. The church is a "holy nation." At first this expression may sound strange to our ears. In our day we use the term "nation" to refer to a country, not to the church. Yet in 1 Peter 2:9 we read: "But you are a chosen race, a royal priesthood, a holy nation, God's own people." These were all terms used in the Old Testament as names for the people of Israel. The terms fit, because the Old Testament people were a nation with geographical boundaries as well as a religious people set apart ("holy").

By calling the church a holy nation, the apostle is bringing a new understanding to this Old Testament usage. While the people of Israel were a nation of one bloodline, the church is a "nation" comprised of people from many nations. While the Old Testament people were bent on claiming nationhood within their own geographical boundary, the church is a "nation" that knows no boundaries. While the Old Testament people desired their earthly king, the church recognizes Christ, the heavenly king, as their supreme head. "No one can lay any foundation other than the one that has been laid; that foundation is Jesus Christ" (1 Corinthians 3:11).

This means that in a way we can still think of the people of God, the church, in political terms. But this "nation" has spiritual dimensions and a spiritual character. The dimensions are bounded by the reign of God. The character of God is manifested in its life. The church is not virtual reality. It has an actual this-worldly dimension with practical implications for daily life.

The church is the spiritual, social and political body that gives its allegiance to God alone. The biblical line of thought, reflected above, influences many aspects of the church's theology, both doctrinal and practical. For example, since the secular government is not our first authority and if the Christian community has an international interest, then it is plain to see why in times of war Christians refuse to fight. To obey and protect the state and its interests is of less importance than to obey Jesus Christ. Furthermore, how can we in good conscience count persons beyond our national borders as our enemies if we consider ourselves to be spiritual citizens of the international community?

It becomes clear why Christians have a concern for mission. We care, in a life-giving way, about all peoples of the earth. We want all people to know the good news that Christ desires to reign in their lives as well. Our first concern is not to protect our own material interests, but to share what we have with others and to receive from others what the Spirit desires to teach us through them. Our vision of the kingdom of God informs our actions: "After this I looked, and there was a great multitude that no one could count, from every nation, from all tribes and peoples and languages, standing before the throne and before the lamb, robed in white, with palm branches in their hands" (Revelation 7:9).

This attitude also means that we look upon no one as less important than ourselves. In secular thinking, political rallies call people to become zealously patriotic for their own country. Sometimes such rallies are inspired at the expense of other countries. For many decades the Western world promoted its importance over against the former USSR. But under God's reign, such political promotion of self does not fit. There are no outsiders; there are no insiders. "So then you are no longer strangers and aliens, but you are citizens with the saints and also members of the household of God" (Ephesians 2:19).

In contrast to the church, governing authorities of the world have been instituted by God for maintaining order in societies. The Anabaptists of the sixteenth century viewed their world in two spheres. In the Schleitheim Confession of 1527, the earliest confession of pre-Mennonite history, these two spheres are called "the law of the sword" and the "perfection of Christ." The "sword" refers to the government. The "perfection of Christ" refers to the kingdom of God which is experienced in and through the fellowship of believers, the church.

The Anabaptists did not tell their people to rebel against the government. Rather they held that we should "be subject to the governing authorities; for there is no authority except from God, and those authorities that exist have been instituted by God" (Romans 13:1). To "be subject" meant to obey the government in all things good. However, if the demands of government conflicted with their covenant with Christ, then Christ must be obeyed.

This still does not permit rebellion or anarchy. "Bless those who persecute you; bless and do not curse them" (Romans 12:14). They believed as it is said in Romans: "Do you wish to have no fear of the authority? Then do what is good, and you will receive its approval" (13:3). When there is an unjust demand upon believers, they should explain their beliefs and be prepared to suffer for what is right.

Yet governments do not always fulfil their calling. It cannot be assumed that they will automatically uphold justice. Indeed, much that goes on in government, as in society generally, is self-seeking and unjust and does not serve the common good. The problem of selfish governance goes back to Adam and Eve who preferred to rule creation on their own rather than to serve

God as their Lord. When Israel requested a king like the other nations (1 Samuel 8), the prophet Samuel was told by God to warn the people of the pitfalls of kingship. They will be tempted to worship their earthly king rather than God (8:7). Still, God allowed the people to have their way (8:19–22).

The glory as well as the shame of kingship is adequately recorded in the Bible and in human history. Ezekiel issues a harsh proclamation against the king of Tyre: "Because you compare your mind with the mind of a god, therefore, I will bring strangers against you. . . . they shall draw their swords against the beauty of your wisdom and defile your splendor" (Ezekiel 28:6–7).

In a similar way, Daniel sets forth the vision of a powerful rising ruler whose glory will in the end by broken "and not with human hands" (Daniel 8:25). The Book of Revelation pictures a powerful ruler who will have authority over the earth and whom all, except the Lord's faithful, will worship. In the end this ruler and the kingdom will be killed by the sword, but the saints will endure (Revelation 13:7–10).

As Christians we are to respect those in authority and to pray for all people, including those in government. What should be our attitude toward governments? The Bible is a remarkably wise guide for us in this respect. In sum, the guidelines are as follows: Be cooperative and obedient citizens of your country. Obey the government in all things which the church discerns as good. Together as a church, you should discern ways of justice. If and when a government requires you to engage in injustice, explain your viewpoint and follow your churchly conscience. This becomes difficult in a country where the government has become despotic. Still, do not create an atmosphere of violence, but continue to speak and act with respect and in love. Maintain a caring and compassionate international perspective. Remember that your first allegiance is to the perfection of Christ, the kingdom of God.

During the Second World War 7,500 Mennonite young adults in Canada registered with the government as conscientious objectors to war. They were allowed to do alternative service such as reforestation, building roads and working in mental institutions. Unfortunately, about 4,500 Mennonite young adults registered for military service at that time.

The Bible urges Christians to pray for their governors. The stated reason for prayer is "so that we may lead a quiet and peaceable life in all godliness and dignity" (1 Timothy 2:2). Our prayer is that the country in which we live and the international community to which we belong might be a peaceful place in which Christians are able to carry on their mission so that the light of Christ may extend to all nations (Isaiah 49:6; Matthew 5:13–16).

We understand that Christ, by his death and resurrection, has won victory over the powers, including all governments. Many times in the history of the Christian church, rulers and their obedient judges and armies have moved ruthlessly against the defenceless and the poor in society. Even in our day much havoc is occurring on every continent of the globe because of the self-interest of power-hungry people. Even countries which appear peaceful are not immune from the struggle, as they are sometimes the suppliers of arms to armies on both sides of the struggle.

Like the Christians who first heard the message of the Book of Revelation, many in our day cry out for a sign that God is still on the throne. Life appears hopeless. Faithful Christians are channels of hope in two ways: in word and in deeds.

The word of hope is based on the story of the resurrection of Jesus from the dead. His death and resurrection have broken the power of final death. Jesus Christ is the resurrected Lord of any and all powers that threaten life, even unto death.

Deeds of hope include feeding the hungry, bringing freedom to people in prison, bringing healing to the physically ill and offering refreshing water to people who are thirsty in body and in soul. These words and actions proclaim that no power can undo the covenant between God and the people of God.

Halleluia! "He disarmed the rulers and authorities and made a public example of them, triumphing over them in it [the cross]" (Colossians 2:15). Halleluia!

Questions for Discussion

1. How is the church understood in article 23? See the first two sections of this chapter and recall chapter 9? What are the key Bible texts that help us with our definition?
2. What is our "theology of government?" That is, what do we believe is God's word about government? Compare Romans 13:1–7 and Revelation 13.
3. How should Christians understand and live out their responsibility toward their governments? What are the implications of voting in elections?
4. What should be the Christian's focal concern in the political realm?

The Reign of God

Do you wonder where life is headed? Your life? Human history? The universe? God created everything for a purpose. The creation of the universe and all that is in it, including humankind, was not a time-bound laboratory experiment or a fun-and-games event that gets dismantled at the end of the day. God had "forever" in mind. We can imagine the lines, "I'll love you forever," written at the head of God's statement of purpose for creation.

We place our hope in the reign of God and in its fulfilment in the day when Christ our ascended Lord will come again in glory to judge the living and the dead. God is reigning now. Where's the evidence? We see signs of God's reign here and there. The cycle of the seasons as well as the rain and sunshine that produce the crops of the field are evidence that God takes care of creation. The cycle of death and birth with the persistent renewal of the earth, including the ongoing generations of the human race, provides further evidence that God reigns. Where despair and discouragement turn to hope and new life, we witness the sustaining grace of God. Where the hungry are fed, the suffering are comforted, the sick are healed, the persecuted are patient, we claim that God reigns.

Even as we point to evidences of the kingdom, we see enough brokenness around us to ask: "Where is the reign of God?" The accumulated pain and suffering upon earth are at times overwhelming. Christian hope looks suffering in the face. At the same time hope overrides hopelessness. We believe God reigns.

How can we make this claim? Above all, on the basis of the death and resurrection and ascension of Jesus Christ. When

Jesus came to earth, he gathered up the hopes and dreams of the people of Israel (Luke 1–2). During his ministry the situation deteriorated and led to his despicable death. The hope of Israel appeared to be dashed to pieces. But then there was the great reversal. God raised Jesus from the dead. This was no illusion. Faithful witnesses gave evidence they had seen the risen Christ. The Christian hope in the eternal reign of God is founded on the historical event of the resurrection of Christ. Our hope rests on this event: that in Jesus, death was turned to new life.

Jesus ascended to be with his heavenly Father (Acts 1). He had said to his disciples: "I will come again and will take you to myself, so that where I am, there you may be also" (John 14:3). When he ascended, the disciples wanted to know if he would establish the kingdom (of Israel) on earth now (Acts 1:6). Jesus deflected the question with the comment that "it is not for you to know the times or periods that the Father has set by his own authority" (1:7). Rather than ponder the dates of the kingdom, the disciples are to witness to what they have seen and heard (1:8). It is right to hope for the consummation of the kingdom of God. Meanwhile, our task is to engage in the works of the kingdom here and now.

We believe that God, who created the universe, continues to rule over it in wisdom, patience and justice, though sinful creation has not yet recognized God's rule. The Creator had something different in mind than what happened early in biblical human history. God would reign over creation, and humans would cooperate in governance of creation by serving God's purposes. A relationship of mutual trust would prevail. This required that humans be endowed with freedom. God could have created robots who would respond to the Creator's bidding with the push of a button. But what kind of a relationship would that have been? God wanted someone with whom to enjoy fellowship and trust. God hoped for a relationship in which humans would want what God wants.

But this did not happen. Adam and Eve abused their privileged freedom. They used it to claim their own superiority over their Creator. Thus they attempted to thwart God's plan. Their sin changed the relationship. The reign of God would continue, but with restrictions placed on humans. The law was necessary to keep them in bounds. An environment with hostile elements surrounded them, reminding them of their limitations. Within this situation God continues to reign.

The Old Testament depicts God's authority and power in interesting and decisive ways. At the parting of the Red Sea to allow the people of Israel to escape from their Egyptian pursuers, God is spoken of this way: "In the greatness of your majesty you overthrew your adversaries; you sent out your fury, it consumed them like stubble. At the blast of your nostrils the waters piled up, the floods stood up in a heap; the deeps congealed in the heart of the sea" (Exodus 15:7–8).

Gideon provides another example. When the people urge him to rule over them, he refuses with the words: "I will not rule over you, and my son will not rule over you; the Lord will rule over you" (Judges 8:23). The sin of Adam had not altogether corrupted the people. God's rule was still respected and anticipated. The prophet Zechariah expressed the hope that at a future final day "the Lord will become king over all the earth" (Zechariah 14:9).

People's response to Jesus shows that the reign of God was not obvious to all. Religious laws and traditions, racial attitudes and political alignments had all but covered up the signs of the kingdom. This is the scene Jesus entered with the announcement: "The time is fulfilled, and the kingdom of God has come near; repent, and believe in the good news" (Mark 1:15). He educated people in the wisdom of kingdom knowledge. His textbook was the Sermon on the Mount (Matthew 5–7).

He spoke and acted with great patience and persistence as he moved from village to village, providing living evidence of the activity of God's reign. In the face of severe criticism he did what was right and he spoke for justice among people. Treating people with fairness and equity was a sign that God reigns. This included offering forgiveness to all people, regardless of religious background or race.

Jesus Christ is Lord. Lord is a ruler's title. God has exalted Jesus to the position of ruler of the kingdom of God. Jesus reigns. But Jesus did not earn his crown through battle. The opposite is the case. "Though he was in the form of God, [he] did not regard equality with God as something to be exploited" (Philippians 2:6). Rather, he "became obedient to the point of death" (2:8). With this qualification Jesus earns our worship. He is the Prince of Peace, the Lamb on the throne. "God has highly exalted him . . . so that . . . every tongue should confess that Jesus Christ is Lord" (2:9–11).

We believe that the church is called to live now according to the model of the future reign of God. Human history continues. Overall, humans do not change their ways of behaving. The freedom given to our first parents is afforded us as well, although with limitations because of the social contexts we inherit from our forebears. The sins of our forebears accumulate as they are repeated in each generation. In the course of this negative development there is much that is positive. Here and there we learn from our mistakes, we take courage in the opportunity for new beginnings and we improve our situation. Yet given the balance of good and evil, of success and failure, life feels like a roller-coaster ride. What goes up comes down and what goes round comes round. Where are we headed?

The Christian faith offers an answer to this ceaseless question. The answer begins with Jesus. He was in a situation where everything he lived for collapsed around him. His disciples had fled. The crowds, who in an earlier day had claimed him as their Messiah, now threw this claim back in his face. His persecutors put him to death and abandoned him to

The Prayer of St. Francis

Lord, make me an instrument of your peace.
  Where there is hatred, let me sow love;
  Where there is injury, pardon;
  Where there is doubt, faith;
  Where there is despair, hope;
  Where there is darkness, light;
  Where there is sadness, joy.
O Divine Master,
  Grant that I may not so much seek
    To be consoled, as to console;
    To be understood, as to understand;
    To be loved, as to love.
  For it is in giving that we receive;
  It is in pardoning that we are pardoned;
  It is in dying that we are born
    to eternal life.

the garbage heap ("Hades"). Then in the face of all this, God raised him from the dead and gave him an exalted place "at the right hand of God" (Acts 2:33).

With this turn of events, a new beachhead was established from which a new era in history was launched. Jesus the risen and exalted Christ is the hope of the world. He offers salvation to all who call on his name (Acts 4:12). Power goes out from him to all who receive forgiveness of sins and attach themselves to him. He becomes the rallying point for the new community, the church. "So if anyone is in Christ, there is a new creation; everything old has passed away; see, everything has become new!" (2 Corinthians 5:17).

The community of the church is formed of persons who profess this message about Jesus Christ, who allow the works of the kingdom of God to transform life's direction and to lure believers toward God's future by the power of hope. Hope functions like a mustard seed (Matthew 17:20–21) in the heart of individual believers and in the heart of the community of faith. We are freed to bloom where we are planted and to scatter the seed of Christian hope abroad in the world. We are driven by the vision of what will be: "Then the seventh angel blew his trumpet, and there were loud voices in heaven, saying, 'The kingdom of the world has become the kingdom of our Lord and of his Messiah, and he will reign forever and ever'" (Revelation 11:15).

We believe that, just as God raised Jesus from the dead, we also will be raised from the dead. Jesus said, "Do not be astonished at this; for the hour is coming when all who are in their graves will hear his voice and will come out—those who have done good, to the resurrection of life, and those who have done evil, to the resurrection of condemnation" (John 5:28–29).

Many people find it hard to believe in a resurrection from the dead. They say they have never seen anything like that. We sometimes hear of someone who was clinically dead, then was resuscitated. But that's not the same as a resurrection. A resuscitated person will die again. The resurrected Jesus will never die. He was raised in a new embodiment, not like his earthly body, although there were some features that continued from his earthly body (the nail prints).

Christians give resounding testimony to the resurrection on the basis of one piece of evidence: Jesus rose from the dead. Support for the evidence is found in at least four directions: 1) trust in the promise and the power of God who raised him; 2) many witnesses who saw the resurrected Jesus; 3) the evidence of the church, the body of Christ, through which the resurrected Christ lives on even to the present day; 4) the final evidence, which will be given when our Lord appears again at the end of this age and the faithful are raised with him.

Meanwhile, faith is the key to our confidence in the resurrection. But our faith is not blind faith. Faith in the resurrected Christ and in our resurrection has a very practical focus. At the end of the apostle Paul's chapter-long discussion of the resurrection, he says: "Therefore, my beloved, be steadfast, immovable, always excelling in the work of the Lord, because you know that in the Lord your labor is not in vain" (1 Corinthians 15:58).

We look forward to the coming of a new heaven and a new earth and a new Jerusalem.

Then I saw a new heaven and a new earth; for the first heaven and the first earth had passed away, and the sea was no more. And I saw the holy city, the new Jerusalem, coming down out of heaven from God, prepared as a bride adorned for her husband. And I heard a voice from the throne saying,

"See, the home of God is among mortals.
He will dwell with them as their God;
they will be his people,
and God himself will be with them;
he will wipe every tear from their eyes.

Death will be no more;
mourning and crying and pain will be no more,
for the first things have passed away."

And the one who was seated on the throne said, "See, I am making all things new" (Revelation 21:1–5).

Questions for Discussion

1. What are the features of the reign of God, according to biblical teaching?
2. Where is the reign of God evident in life today in the midst of a sinful world?
3. What is the role of the church in keeping alive the reality and the hope of the kingdom (reign) of God?
4. What part does the resurrection of Jesus contribute to an understanding of God's reign? What is meant by "walking in the resurrection" (Romans 6:4)?
5. Share ways in which the hope of God's final victory, as stated in Revelation 21:1–5, plays a role in your daily faith.

Quotations

Page viii. Michael Sattler, in John Howard Yoder, *The Legacy of Michael Sattler* (Scottdale: Herald Press, 1973), 114, 115.

Page viii. Hans Denk from "Recantation," in Walter Klaassen, ed., *Anabaptism in Outline* (Scottdale: Herald Press, 1981), 46.

Page 16. Peter Riedeman from "Account," in Walter Klaassen, ed., *Anabaptism in Outline* (Scottdale: Herald Press, 1981), 77–78.

Page 46. Menno Simons from "Christian Baptism," in J.C. Wenger, ed., *The Complete Writings of Menno Simons* (Scottdale: Herald Press, 1956, 1984), 265.

Page 88. Menno Simons, quoted in *A Mennonite Polity for Ministerial Leadership* (Newton: Faith & Life Press, 1996), 11.

Page 97. "The Apostles' Creed," quoted in *Hymnal: A Worship Book* (Elgin: Brethren Press; Newton: Faith & Life Press; Scottdale: Mennonite Publishing House, 1992), #712.

Page 110. Menno Simons from "True Christian Faith," in J.C. Wenger, ed., *The Complete Writings of Menno Simons* (Scottdale: Herald Press, 1956, 1984), 396.

Page 124. Daniel Kauffman, *Managers with God: Continuing the Work Christ Began* (Scottdale: Herald Press, 1990), 40.

Page 133. David Toews, quoted in Frank H. Epp, *Mennonites in Canada 1786–1920: The History of a Separate People* ([Altona]: Mennonite Historical Society of Canada, 1974), 381.

Page 148. "Prayer of St. Francis of Assisi."